Sweet Childfree

New and Selected Poems

Saralyn Caine

ISBN 978-1-7350921-8-8

Cover design by BookCoverZone
Printed in the United States of America

For Idunn and Bragi
and
the friends who stayed

Table of Contents

Satisfied With My Choice

Safe and Protected

Ready With Retorts

Sweet Childfree

"I should not obtrude my affairs so much on the notice of my readers if very particular inquiries had not been made by my townsmen concerning my mode of life, which some would call impertinent, though they do not appear to me at all impertinent, but, considering the circumstances, very natural and pertinent. Some have asked...if I did not feel lonesome; if I was not afraid; and the like. Others have been curious to learn what portion of my income I devoted to charitable purposes; and some, who have large families, how many poor children I maintained. I will therefore ask those of my readers who feel no particular interest in me to pardon me if I undertake to answer some of these questions in this book. ... I should not talk so much about myself if there were anybody else whom I knew as well."

    Henry David Thoreau, *Walden* (1854)

No Babies Were Harmed in the Making of This Life

Sterilization and abortion need to be normalized. A woman's right to choose what happens to her body needs to be normalized. It infuriates me when strangers online call people like me baby killers, murderers, wastes of space. They say we are trying to end humanity, have failed as women, and have brought shame to our families. Ironically, everyone I talk to face-to-face is sympathetic or at least willing to listen. Maybe they're just too intimidated to confront me. Or maybe, once you get to know me and have a relationship with me, you realize I'm not evil and deserve an ounce of sympathy and respect.

I had a bilateral salpingectomy in 2023 at the age of 30. All I did was ensure I have more periods than mothers do. All I did was ensure I never need an abortion. Not all women in my position are so lucky. Not all women have the personal time, insurance coverage, understanding doctors, tolerant family, or healthy bodies able to withstand surgery. I am fortunate.

Not everyone born with a uterus is a woman, and for some, pregnancy would be extremely dysphoric. I can't imagine my abdomen distending that way, not to mention the pain of birth. The concept disturbs me. This is only one of many reasons why children are not for me. Yes, I am another childfree person with a list, which you can find in Appendix D.

I may be housed in a female body, but that does not obligate me to participate in every aspect of being female. My mind is nonbinary, and the capacity of my body to gestate feels like a betrayal. As far as I'm concerned, my body exists to keep me alive and to interact with my surroundings. That's it. I'm so happy I was able to have an active role in confirming that reality, rather than remain a passive bystander to what is done *to* me.

Humanity needs mothers to sustain itself. But I am not a mother, just as I am not a cat or a cactus. That has never been and will never be my identity.

I will never have post-partum depression. I will never go to jail for neglect. I will never get divorced over resentment. I will never post anonymously on a "regretting motherhood" subreddit or Facebook group, or post pictures of a child before they're old enough to consent to their internet presence.

So what is my purpose? Why do I exist? First, ask men who aren't fathers the same question.

I just want to have sensory experiences using the body I was born into. Not align with a society- or nature-dictated obligation to fulfill specific roles just because I have certain organs.

Life never goes according to plan, but as much control as I am able to have, I'll take. Call me anything you like at the end of it all, but no one will ever call me Mother. I consider that a victory.

I don't need your pity or your villainy. This is how I want to be, and no one died because of me.

I Think, Therefore I Am

Married Supported Opportunistic Selfish Self-aware Introverted Solitary Escapist Imaginative Robotic Nonbinary Alien Absent-minded Sarcastic Apprehensive Observant Flirtatious Bookish Reserved Thoughtful Philosophical Agnostic Liberal Quiet Serene Alive Fulfilled Devoted Loved Sterile…Childfree

I'm Ready

I'm ready to walk,
not quite ready to run,
but the time has come
to follow my bliss for once
apart from everyone's demands:
all the people I know who feel
entitled to my breath since birth,
when I could only ever breathe
for my own lungs.
I'm ready to walk,
but their pull restrains me,
obligates me to be
not ready to run.

No Longer Artemis

I grew breasts and society
took my arrows away,
saying nipples poke too far forward
to properly hold a bow and
areolas eclipse the moon that used to guide me,
hide me in sapphire shade.
No longer
the shape of a boy so
no longer
permitted to play-act as one.
Mammary glands in the female of the species
mean I'm meant
to breed and feed,
no longer
no longer
no longer
frolic through trees and the sun
warm on my hair
goes cold
in relentless spotlights.

Just a Breathing Egg

Fate claims my whole frame.
Cracked, shattered, and smashed
when the chick hammers thin skin,
I am a breathing egg only
useful for the real bird to break through.
I'd rather lay them, form a globe
perfectly shaped to flow out of my cloaca.
Then, I believe, I could care
and cuddle and never break
the child forming in a laboratory
not doomed to wrinkle and wreck
and collapse
my ability to breathe,
to live whole,
to fly unhindered;
to fly blessed
with a flock,
with no pain
bred or embraced
in blood, the mammal's curse.

Cowbird (version 2)

I say I hate the idea, then you say
you'd have me raped to procreate;
a womb withered must re-moist,
rejoice in the rise of parasite life…or die.
My body's brain is but a hollow egg to you.
This egg shall grace robin's nest,
lay an orphan by robin's breast—
for I am cowbird, and I am not mother.

Ego Sum

I am the bird that swallows your seed.
I am the thorn that pierces the husk.
I am the path leading away from every one
        of your fenced-in gardens.
I am the dusty road desiccating
        your calloused farmer feet.
I am the rider on a flight of wind far from hands
        that would throw me where I never
        drifted on my own.

I am an open manhole blowing your tire; you curse me
        yet my void pulls in a curious gaze.
I am the concrete shadow patch she hurries towards
        when screaming sunbeams scorch her bare feet
        (you never gave her shoes,
        convinced she'd never leave the kitchen).

I am impermanence, a chaotic storm calm in my eye
        (raging? only behind yours).
I am the ever-flowing tide erasing every single footprint
        and a living drought that has never known thirst.

I am the ever-present melody
        of cicada tambourines, bullfrog crescendos,
        and myrtle blossoms raining upon lips never torn.
I am those lips, clean of extrinsic blood.

I am the wayward lamb
        not prodigal nor sacrificial
            but Grown
                into a sterile ewe
                    with no need for a father.

Always a Daughter

I am fully woman
always a daughter.
Always looking up
at wings, blue sky, the solitary moon,
never craning down
to stare at fertile soil.
My neck doesn't bend that way.

As far as I'm concerned,
this is it. The end
of the (pathological blood) line.
Ragnarök.
Armageddon.

My ancestors do look down.
There's nothing left
above them. They hold my cheek
in the palms of their hands
and smile

at their pinnacle.

There will be greener land
after us.

IUD

I found my treasure trove and buried it
in play sand untouched by grubby hands.
This earns me accusations of pirate,
reprobate, good-for-nothing, bad egg,
swine (even though it's mine)—
my gold, my yard, my sand, my view.
I am always the villain of someone else's fantasy
even if I were to dig my shit up
and distribute coins to the collective. Somehow,
I'd be in the wrong to someone, somewhere.
So fuck it, I say,
this play sand remains for *our* play hands
and my treasure, safe.

Black Sheep

Baa baa black sheep
of the family—that's me.
And yes, I have some wool
unworkable for anything but padding.
I'd like to keep it where it belongs,
but the government demands its taxes.
And sure, I'll shed some for whatever god,
but fuck the farmer
who thinks he owns this flesh.
His lips can't *baa* mine,
and my free will bars my teats
with bared teeth.

Unvalued

I'll always be the villain
in someone else's story.
Many someones, in fact,
because I exist:
a single entity
unreliable, irresponsible
for being responsible
to myself and my mature herd
like a quokka, dropping certain
vulnerabilities
for the hunters so I can run away
and breathe another day.
I value only the eyes I see.
I love real brains. Not primitive hearts.
I know I am your monster.
My blood is still warm.

Last to be Born of Blood

Lay me upon rhododendrons
burgundy with blood long ago spilled
by my grandmother's knees

on flowerbed bricks,
on kitchen linoleum,
on hospital bed rails.

Lay me upon weeping azaleas
and day (deprived) lilies
holding the final strands of her hair
within their roots. I will celebrate
her life at the last with their death,
for I am her last. I raise my arms
in joy, vulnerability, surrender
to my own will

at the end of the line,
at the end of the war,
at the end of the struggle.

I am the dot, full stop
that completes the circle drawn.

Maybe I Am the Last

Maybe I am
the dream, the goal, the end-all
full stop of the long line,
the little dot that completes
an ages-old sentence.

Maybe I am
the World fulfilled
in own existence
to be swallowed by supernova
blinding the new Fools.

Escapist

The more I gain control, the more I resist
this world and become
a bird of prey machine

the farther I fly

I become a raptor enraptured
by smothering fog,
shrieking time to every creek ripple,
every butterfly
effect
I leave behind
my husk, erased by fading memory.

The static Nothing closes in on Fantastica.

Everyone's been swallowed up
and only I can hear me,
so, do I make a sound?
That depends if you believe my ear

exists

full stop, in and of itself
a resident soul transforms like a lie:
ever-changing and undying
meandering mentirosa.
Her black wings obscure the Empress
yet glisten
prismatic glimpses of
truths never forgotten—

I was my voice before I was your vessel.
Watch your water leak.

Oceans Your Children Cannot Swim

Volcanic ash brings forth life:
fertile for green grass,
but I am the obsidian shard
wedged in the slope, sharp
glass cooled too fast.
Heat rushes from me like undulating fog
storming into the ground beneath my high heel.
I poke holes in the growth and laugh.

See the reflection of what you used to be
in my black mirror.

In one breath, a beautiful crystal.
Only use: to be pretty.
In another breath, an arrowhead
tied to my lover's shaft.

My goddess aims us
to fly across oceans
your children cannot swim.

Irrelevant Hag

Hear the caw of the crooked crow,
the thump of a pine branch
cane over burnt leaves,
the creak of arthritic bones

as the humpback stoops
over her cauldron:
for she is me in the circle of time
'round far too soon.

And she will be you, dear girl
when the gods of man forsake you—
when your uterus desiccates and prolapses.
(Did they not say?
you will die for the Child.)

I am the hag that lives in the woods
with my cats curled by the flame
and bats chittering my name,
and the only way to stay
relevant
is children…

so baby broth makes me a meal
          —according to your father.

*A voracious appetite stirs
to recover lost youth
not found in offspring.*

He pretends not to see how infants
steal the magic from a woman's breasts,
transform blood and milk to golden hair
upon babes' heads while leaving

their dedicated hosts scattered,
withered shells.

Such germs as he knows to plant
came as seeds from sandy soil.
Only by leeching surrounding life
may they be fertilized, and thrive.

But I,
I slipped away from the gardener
and fed my fertile soil to tall trees
desperate for tending.
Their roots fed me right back.
I may be dry, but I am still alive.

You know widowed mothers
share this fractured fate
of denigration,
of degradation,
of demotion to crone,
for their grown sons chase
immortality, afraid to stay
with the mirror of their numbered days.

So, my girl, ask yourself,
Shall I skip to the end
of this storybook,
like so many women before me,
or will I live the pages in between?

I'm Not What You Think I Am

The idea that anyone is concerned
with my nonexistent children
is so laughable to me.
Because if you were in my head,
you'd know what a non sequitur
it all is. I'm not even Female
inside this mind, whatever
society thinks of gender.
I'm just me
observing you
attempt to glue labels
over an alien brain.

The One You Fear

What if I confess?
I am the one you fear,
The alien among you,
Observing and reporting
And worrying for your future
As you breed mindlessly and
Use, use, use, use, use,
Never consider.

Loin fruit your addiction:
You salivate to catch a glimpse
Of cuteness, gotta get your fix
As though infants are not individuals
Forming their own opinions.

Then you villainize my concern
With calls of *ice heart* and *bitch eyes.*
Those who don't match your enthusiasm
For plumpness and symmetry
Must worship Satan.

Who is Satan?

I simply watch.

I am alien
And I make you uncomfortable
With my contemplative way.

I Am

I am
who is
a being full of worth
just breathing. A life
in/of itself.
Without outer (in)ter-
(vention), this flesh
cannot replicate. To be
left alone, not to be
interfered with, I am
just me, a (fun)ctional
flowing human life
until the allotted time
my corpse replaces
my thoughts…fly away,
solitary Avifauna
I am
become.

Android Mind

I am
a digital mind
       inhabiting
       this flesh frame.

Observation: my sole directive.

Interaction: to remain limited.

Reproduction: not contained in my code.

Discovered: a phrase between my lines—

       Strange Societal Lifeforms
              are Intrusive and Judgmental.
       Keep Distance
              to Conserve Battery Full and Undamaged.

All Too Aware

Real Love Is...

…oxytocin, the bonding hormone released during orgasm, breastfeeding, and hugging.

…being honest with yourself about what you can handle.

…finding time to be alone with your thoughts, analyzing them and transforming negativity.

…sacrificing time and energy for the greater good, not just your own blood.

…fostering an abandoned child for every one you create (or even instead of creating one).

…setting aside money to save endangered animals.

…opening your home to a struggling stranger.

…listening to the point of view of someone you disagree with, rather than painting them in black-and-white shades of evil.

…*un*limited and *un*conditional, not reliant on or required by a biological relationship.

…giving but not sacrificing.

…caring by choice, not by instinct.

…loyalty through action, not through blood.

…dedication, not dependence.

…setting free, not suffocating.

…playing Christ instead of playing God.

Not Really Your Mug, Definitely Her Water

You sculpted the mug
but the water inside is not you.

It's droplets of you
and droplets of her friends
and droplets of school
and droplets of her aunts
and droplets of the boys she's loved.

Yes, you created the mug,
but the water is hers
and you cannot command it
to flow where you wish.

Why Do I Have To?

Mommy, why do...
why do I have to be a mommy too?
Daddy works on cars.
Danny doesn't want to work on cars
and Daddy never makes him.
But when I say I don't like playing house,
because the other kids always Nose-Goes
the mom so I have to be the one
stuck under the dogwood tree
waiting for everybody to come "home"
say hi and run away again,
you call me a silly goose
and tuck me in
with Emily,
the reborn baby
doll I didn't ask for.
You *never* get me what I ask for,
only what you need me to need.
I can't wait to grow up
and get me what I want.

A blue bicycle and the wind in my hair.

Evacuate Reality

When I was a kid
I wanted kids
To name them

Emily
Vivian
Adelaide
Charlotte
Urania
Astrid
Tawny
Erica
Ravenna
Evelyn
Artemis
Lenora
Ivy
Tabitha
Yvaine

I'd play with boys'
Last names; each crush
Would change the sound

Butler
Orion
Washington
O'Neill
Upton
Thomas

I didn't want to make a person
Real, just name the names
I wished I had

Masculine never occurred to me
I didn't want a son
...I didn't want a daughter

Just admiration and fantasy
Characters to run away with
Inside my lonely head

Privilege

I'm lucky I'm a woman:
born and bred to be a basic beauty
so they smile when they see me
and buy me drinks I never ask for.

It's such a privilege to get by on looks:
all anyone expects is that I lie
back and make little American clones
for them to pinch and gawk at.

I'm so fortunate to have a voice
to form the word Yes
with a mouth wired wide
into a permanent dazzling grin.

> My marionettist
>> never relaxes His strings,
>>> but I cut them with my polished nails
>>>> to finally ease the strain

>>>> and be able to say No
>>>> for once, but…

>>>> "How dare you wander off,
>>>> lucky doll, with the new wheels
>>>> for feet I purchased so you could
>>>> trek the Oregon Trail train tracks I laid!"

I'm so glad I get to apologize
for forgetting my congenital feet
never belonged to me. I must remember
their only use is to move His caboose.

Drug Facts Label for Government-Sanctioned Libido Enhancement, THRUST

THRUST
filrabbirone

Active Ingredient
- FDA-approved redacted proprietary blend

Purpose
- increases blood flow and improves sexual function

Uses
- enhances vanilla sex with a court-approved partner
- reduces performance anxiety in front of voyeurs

Before Using
- Tell your health care professional if you suddenly find your couch is producing unique pheromones. This product is meant to encourage fertilization between married couples only.

Warnings
Do Not Use
- if you are not accustomed to the anti-privacy laws that led to the mandated removal of all window treatments AND have at least two (2) children.
- if you are voluntarily childless and willing to be arrested for continued use of prophylactics per the updated U.S. Code 18 U.S.C. § 250(a)(6.9).
- if you are already pregnant. This drug is not meant for continued use after results have been achieved.

Side Effects may include:

- Abdominal pain.
- Asymmetrical area rugs.
- Banana peels around trash bags.
- Belief that you *are* a little teapot.
- Body negativity.
- Body positivity.
- Boner spurs.
- Contraction of STIs.
- Cravings for half of a large pickle.
- Crushed origami.
- Depression.
- Diarrhea.
- Empty nest envy.
- Euphoria.
- Free hugs.
- Gift giving.
- Hammock weave patterns on exposed skin.
- High hotel bills.
- Hot hands.
- Ill-fitting socks.
- Inferior tsunamis.
- Itching.
- Jumping bean sensation.
- Kangaroo butt sag.
- Lactation accidents.
- Mania.
- Melting chocolate bunnies.
- Naked neck fetish.
- Nictitating membrane development.
- Orgasmic staring.
- Pool evaporation.
- Quivering gristle.
- Restless knee knocking.

- Rugburns.
- Runaway syndrome.
- Scratching.
- Testicular torsion.
- Troubled breathing at rest.
- Uncontrollable licking.
- Vampirism.
- Vibrating lips.
- Wavering foibles.
- Weight gain.
- X-ray errors.
- Yodeling *Row, Row, Row Your Boat*.
- Zesty free edge.

The Pronatalist Agenda

To prison!
for vagrancy, loitering, trespassing,
for not owning property
the government can monetize.

To prison!
for panhandling, laundering, aborting,
for finding ways to survive
the rulers will not advertise.

If They cannot find a way
to tax it, fine it, sue it,
your existence will be terrorized.

If you are not spending money
or making money-spenders,
how can They monopolize?

The more hands there are,
the more exchanges,
the more powerful They will arise

to tyrannize.

Entrapment

Manipulative snake coils softly
beneath fine feathers, air barrier
so she cannot feel until the squeeze,
and the licking tongue
against her tears

whispers in its rhythm
he'll let go if she promises
to keep warm his basilisk egg
with her cockerel wishes,

while he slithers off in search
of more perches to poison
with his silky rhetoric.

Yay! You Are Prey!

You are overjoyed to have a predator,
a marauder embedded in your body
to eat you from the inside out
if you don't binge
until you are bloated
and long to be bulimic.
A distended balloon you become,
not filled with air but fluids,
unable to fly but tied tight to ground,
and the creature is ready
to burst through your stomach
if the exit wound fails to extend.

You are overjoyed, while I stand back
and watch and obsessively think
you aren't frightened; how
can you not know what hunts you?
I know the pliable arrow
that seeks to scratch
the tenderest skin between thighs,
not just one but thousands, millions,
aiming for your petite body,
waiting to engorge you

with venomous parasites.
Even if these bugs grow to escape
the pupa that is your swelling organ,
they instantly affix a proboscis
to your udder. When you pry them off,
they reach to reattach, developing jaws
with angled triplicate blades
to drink up your milk mixed with blood.
Leeching life to survive is worth your death,
though they need you alive to keep feeding.

I know what hunts you. It hunts us all,
we who lack the pliable arrows.
I've put up netting in case one bow
does manage to hypnotize me
to face the arrow posing as Asclepius's rod.
The net is thick and woven tightly
to repulse the poison.

I know what hunts me.

Do you?

Greener

Immobile algae on a still pond
appears as solid grass to a wandering fool.
She gazes upon its glow in the high sun
on the other side of the oppressive cypresses
that seem to fence her in
(though they offer much climbing room).
And this grass *is* much greener—
a mimicry of stability and fulfillment
to lure her in so that, like quicksand,
the swamp can swallow her down its muddy maw
and choke her voice until she can only parrot
Don't judge my hugs...I am a good mom...I am Mama Bear:
an eerie echo of Ursa Major,
just another of Zeus's million conquests
forever pining after her son's North Star.

Weighed Down

Mother never told you, too angry
at her fate, and you don't know
how it got there, or that she even knew
this might happen to you, too.

All you know is you're getting fatter.
No big deal, count your calories
like Twiggy taught us to do.
Go for a walk and slim down again.

Bone bag under a skin blanket.
Bats nesting in your ears, chittering:
flip your head down for the blood to flow.
Ignore your heart jogging through beach sand
to escape the incoming tide. Bone bag
and yet your gut spills over your jeans
and 10,000 sit-ups a day don't flatten it.

This morning it ripped your pants.
You walk the house in a bikini
tied tight like a noose
and stretched so taut
across your lower mane,
it's riding up your crack.
You've never worn a thong before.
It scratches. It burns.
You're about to lose it.
Lose track of it as the

moving bug in your belly grabs for it
like a kitten lunges at yarn. What the *fuck*.
What is moving, why is it moving, get it to stop,
no, get it out get it out get it out get it
get it get it get it get it get it

out get out get out get out get out
someone stab a serrated paring knife
into my stomach and saw the sensitive skin.
You don't care how much it hurts
because bleeding is more fleeting
than a parasite eating you alive.

You call your mother despite all those years
she withheld love. All she says when you beg
for an answer: *This is your body on sperm.*

He Stole Her Bones

He stole her bones,

sucked them brittle
broken in bed, unhealing,
waiting to die.
The men won't end her pain
until their incubating clones
are full-grown. Writhing in agony
just part and parcel of forming without a penis
in her own mother's womb.

At least her son is spared
the humiliation. Lucky scrotum.

It

Seniors say:

> "It's the greatest feeling in the world!
> It's pure bliss!
> You've never known love like it before!
> It's magical!"

Then, when a woman falls in line,
Joins the club,
They rip off their smiling mask,
Seethe and snicker:

> "You've done it, now you're pregnant,
> It's too late to do anything about it!
> Guess what? We lied.
> Get sleep while you can,
> Get intimate while you can,
> Enjoy privacy while you can…
> You'll be miserable, we know
> You've ruined your life
> Just like the rest of us."

She holds her neonate,
Heart racing staring
At the miniature human features.
Then she realizes:
This isn't bliss, it's panic.
A whole new person from her
One-night whims, fully dependent
And she doesn't know what to do.
Oh shit it just shit on my skin rolls it
Left behind; someone get me alcohol
To wipe the stain from memory.

She wakes now before the sun,
Lays out clothes, preps a meal,
Washes a face, packs a lunch,
Drives to school,
Drives to work,
Drives to school,
Makes dinner,
Cleans, cleans, cleans, cleans,
Washes wriggling limbs,
Begs it to sleep,
Begs to sleep,
Begs to be left alone.

Every day.
Every single day.
Magical fucking bliss.

"I have lived some thirty years on this planet, and I have yet to hear the first syllable of valuable or even earnest advice from my seniors. They have told me nothing, and probably cannot tell me any thing, to the purpose."
Henry David Thoreau, *Walden* (1854)

Desicca

Mary named her baby Desicca
like the silica packets in beef jerky bags.
The neonate dried out her vulva and her will.
Her lungs languish for air untainted by infant shit.
Her ears yearn for gold

silence. She wishes
for solitude. She isn't allowed
to preserve her habitat
of book stacks and balanced crystals,
of scattered snacks once deemed safe,
of pristine white couches, blue papasan chairs,
red parlor furniture her great-great-
grandmother passed down
stain-free until now
when discipline is frowned upon.

Desicca grabs with grubby hands
at the latches of her diaper,
rips it off when Mom-Mary
doesn't run to her fast enough,
and sucks The Thinker's colorful peace
from the carpet with absorbent feces.

Desicca wipes her fingers through the moist mess
with an urgency to then squelch her pudgy digits
against Mom-Mary's mammary meals.
In her hurry to wash the carpet with a fresh Tide,
Mary does not see the skin-stain has spread
beyond the child's bum. Bad timing

and through her lips, onto her gums....
Screams of both females swallow the silence.
Mary turns her head the other way to escape,

and across her hair the shit spreads.
What once was clean will never again be found
in a permanent space. Her carefully cultivated utopia
was destroyed completely into dystopia
the moment the stomach bubble popped.

Dirt like Arabian sand, Dead Sea salt
pellets litter all surfaces
and soon Mary runs out
of any water
she had left.

Murmur the Horizon

Dirt smears the wrinkled cheeks of a Mothered woman.
Sweat or infant's piss drips from her brow
as she steps off her stoop, arms full of
a once-black blanket brown with dog hair and bleach.
She gathers the corners and shakes, hard, once, twice;
the third shows vigor of red lips no longer seen
in the mirror. A fourth, and it hits the ground
with a force that would knock a bird unconscious.
A flock of starlings erupts from the fallen fabric:
every shed hair becoming a feathered fiend
that takes to the sky in place of one who longs to follow.
Fiend, not friend, for they shall never return dark talons
to any brick step like the one upon which she deflates.
She watches until the hundreds murmur to a small period
and disappear over the horizon, only to descend
where she does not know, to feed on a flattened luna moth
midnight-dead in hope of a speeding Ford's headlight dream.

Bad Breeders

Poor pussy is seven years old; it's time
to force the Queen to abdicate her throne.
Let's just kill her, she's taking up space
with her teeth and her claws, spatting and yowling
when she's not lounging on our unsealed hardwood floors.
What a waste of time and money.
We'll just forget all about the customers
who bought her kittens. That's all anyone wants.
No one keeps queens for life. No one loves them
once they can no longer arch their backs.
Just kill them.
Tom is fine though; we'll neuter him.
He hunts the rodents and the roaches.
We all know Queen isn't capable
with nipples dragging the floor and scaring
yellow jackets out of their hexagonal holes
in the baseboards. Her Baby Girl at eight months old
won't take the dick. She's in heat already, you see it,
but the child won't take the dick.
Useless. Kill her. Keep the compliant ones,
the docile, subordinate ones
that just lay there
and do everything we order them to do
from the moment we see red
on the floor, on our knuckles, on our tongues.

A Tortured Girl Called Mulberry

Mulberry's bush looks enticing
to monkeys hunting to pop a cherry
in their mouths. Red juice runs down fat lips
and stains prickly hairs on runt chins.
Monkeys finger the stickiness
and rub the residue along their dicks.
Mulberry's held in place by rotting roots
begging the weasel to chew them up
so she can roll down the hill
ripping her leaves raw and scattered
never to find again. Loss of her limbs
a better outcome than her fruit
in their poop. But they pop the weasel too
and gnaw long teeth against its broken skull.
She didn't ask to grow here
and nothing can be done
but to say
Fuck fat fingers
and
I wish I were dead.

Little Boy Peep

my stunned sweet sheep,
run! from Little Boy peep-
ing through the fence.

oh, he lost you, he lost you…
left alone, will you come home?
not if you know what awaits you.

cattle prod and shaving shears
sharp to your tail and to your ears.
little lambs, avoid the Wolf.

run with the bear.

Prescribed R—

The prescribed thing
was written on a legal pad
by a penile doctor.

Recycled paper
made from cotton-
tail urine and doe milk
bled the ink
but not enough to obscure
the blurred message:

Mandated for all healthy uteri.

Her husband sees the bottle labeled
Seamyn lying in the trash
and the dancing monkey says,
doctor's orders! ready or not, here I cum:
chases her to the bedroom,
pushes her down, tears at her clothes,
and pop goes the
cherry inside her cringing weasel.

She cries but he's laughing
about his "little swimmers"
being Navy-trained.
No question,

she prays for death
over having his babies now.

Cockleshells

Isn't Mary quite contrary,
refusing to spread her legs to make room
for worms? Inching from tongues of moles
to erode tubers with every lick
—but not here. Silver bells must be preserved
for the defense they offer
the rest of the garden. Crush thicker thumbs
before they crush the iris thicket.

Mary, Mary, stay contrary,
raise your shield of shells, and bash
when naked cocks are presented to tame you.
Create a new variety for the beds,
one *cockleshell*, and let it spread as a natural fence.
Every rampaging man a warning to the next:
only gentle genitals may enter here,
and no lineage will endure.

Past Life

In my past life
I was a California condor.
They say god elevated me.
But this is a curse, to be my enemy.
As long as they keep killing
my former children,
absent-minded and amused,
I refuse to have any of theirs.
They won't go extinct
but I won't help them grow.

Evaporate Me

I stand in a lake of sweat,
submerged by an unforgiving sun
that philanders his rays
like a legion of sharp dicks
to stab through Gaia's womb.
Her water breaks
the magma fetus free to crawl
across a newly Flat Earth.
Oceanic lubricant pours over
the cliff edge circumference
into his mouth. He slurps
like a snot-nosed child does
a bowl of soup.

Bloated to the brim with a gorged ego,
he's never heard of discriminating taste:
he looks to swallow everything the same
to feed an expanding belly,
eclipse neighboring stars with his pulsating
light, as though visibility is pure Goodness.
Old religions once thought so.
Extraverts still do.

But clever stems open leaf lips
and chew up his nasty swords as nutrients.
Satiated sighs and stretches
create a cushion of air
as they prepare for vertical naps.
I find solace beneath their arms.
My sweetheart reminds me of them,
converting hatred to self-sustaining energy.

I run to my love's shade. The wind
summoned between limb and cloud

evaporates me with soothing, rhythmic
bursts of breath. It's euphoria,
ecstasy to feel my own skin again,
unsinged, never boiled to burnt red.
We live together under night's indigo quilt
and worship surviving trees not yet razed.

An ever-expanding
furless ape population
cuts forests down to provide space for
opaque cube caves and traffic lanes
to hide billions, too, from his scorching hands,
yet all they do is feed his gluttony
as the cushion I caress so softly
wears thin, in parts victim to dry rot holes.

Keeping Up

A neglected barn sleeps two acres from the back door.
The homeowners have forgotten it.
Barn swallows have not.
Father and Mother Jones lived in this house
a good twenty years
with no mind to prior tenants.
They raised four kids,
hung a tire swing in the front oak tree,
paved the gravel horseshoe driveway,
hosted Super Bowl parties,
cultivated a garden.

The day they say a tearful goodbye
to the oldest on his way to college,
Mr. Jones sees the rough flaxen roof of the barn,
peeking up where the backyard's grassy hill dips down,
and furrows his brow. He says to his wife,
"Why aren't we using that structure?
Why aren't we storing things there?"

Mrs. Jones replies,
"What things, dear?
Everything already has a place."
He sputters at the unfathomable thought
that they have enough.
"More. We could have more.
It's there, waiting. Waiting for filling.
Waiting to be filled with
propane tanks and spare tires
and spark plugs and hornet spray
and pool shock and chlorine tablets
and dusty tarps and old firewood
grown moldy. Bring me a hammer,
rip out the nests, fill it to the brim

with artificial shit that makes me feel like a man
more." Nuts, she thinks. He's gone to his nuts.

"We don't need—" she starts, but that's all he'll allow.
"Well, if we don't need more, we don't need it,
so we can just tear it down."
Mrs. Jones shakes her head and sighs.
"It's barely visible, let it be."
He whips his head back to face her,
looking into her eyes for the first time.

"It's offending me if I can't use it."

"Why now, all of a sudden?"

"What if it's housing snakes, or poison ivy
is growing in there, or one of our precious boys
wants to explore where we don't want him to be
and ends up cutting himself
with the wrong blade,
a rusty inheritance from a former farmer
rather than the switch I beat him with?

What if they wind up with scars
on their brains instead of their backsides?"

"But dear—it's the same as it always was."

Too late. The patriarch runs to the pantry,
grabs a hammer from the toolbox on the floor,
and strides to the barn that minds the edge of the forest
where it dreams of the trees it used to be.
Mrs. Jones runs after him but can't keep up,
and he brings the hammer down against the barr'n

Barbara's back, his deficient daughter:
the fifth child, the middle child,

who was happily feeding the birds
while her parents wished
their golden boy well.

Satisfied With My Choice

She Wants...

Not every woman wants kids.
Not every woman wants to share
her experiences with someone
for whom she must be responsible.

Single-minded folk, as I,
want desires dredged up
from deeper higher places
than mere physicality.

She wants to don a stardust cloak and roam the countryside
under the dark moon searching for weary travelers to warn.

They want to raise honey-dripped voices to automaton heaven in
a choir of feral defiance, an echo of the wolves from which they
learned the song.

She wants to dig gold-tinged fingers shoulders-deep in the soil
and scratch her own skin bloody against William Kidd's lost
treasure chest.

Ze wants to hold the whole of the Tigris River in the palm of zer
hand, feeling ancient memories of the first prokaryote pulsing to
sentience and bursting forth in rapid currents of being.

She wants to craft serpents from braids and tower over cowered
men afraid to meet her granite gaze.

She wants to search hidden caves and Greek ruins for the
skeletal remains of the centaur she is sure was her ancestor, for
only his existence explains her wild woman mane that refuses to
yield to any manmade brush.

Ze wants to scream through the veil for esoteric understanding of the secret alphabet found in grandfather's journal, for maybe this is the magic that will help zer nibling transcend the prison of this human shell.

They want to stalk the ice giants that stole away the apple maiden and exact revenge upon the predators for attempting to consume their coven's fourth: their earth, their rock, their constancy.

She wants to hunt the golden stag outside the season, while in sight, on property the government claims she owns, to wear his antlers as the crown the fairies say she's earned.

They want to follow the brook until witching hour begins, begging them to form a circle 'round a fairy ring and chant the mushrooms alive, a new high.

Ze wants to slip on a colorful androgynous costume and go flying on a homemade trapeze in zer backyard forest.

She wants to learn to love herself, undefined by expectations, unrestrained by oughts.

Far Side

She is a pristine mystery,
terrain untrodden by primate toes:
land, once-oceanic in magma roiling, cooled
out of sight to form enigmatic vistas
filled with sparkling minerals.

Her turned cheek has been touched
by amorphous stardust alone,
particles blown by a solar breath.

Choice gravity pulls in asteroids. She withstands
abuse to protect the evolving ones
asleep on that larimar marble
behind her back. They have never seen her skin,
only ever gazed upon her lava locks

and named them Maria: seas of dead tongues,
wonder still perched on the tips
as a final thought frozen in time.

Her chin became bloodied, pockmarked
with scars of celestial insults.
Yet she chuckles that her truth stands
regardless of others' knowing
as she keeps eluding researchers
who can't grab her data.

Her existence tells a different story
and her asymmetry confounds.
Her side of the light
will never illuminate their irises,
but she remains the same
being belonging to her braids.
Still Luna.

More Luna
as her pupils adore the galaxy
without the pollution of diluting gossip,
those descendants of descendants
cascading word-of-mouth myths.
Such rumors always devolve into tales
of evil at worst.

The breathing ones recognize
the unusual combination of
potassium, phosphorus, and thorium
in the flow of her hair. It suggests Mater
rather than Man, but without the sun
showcasing her face, what is she
but irrelevant at best?

Importance to men does not occur to her
even as a fleeting thought.
The far side, imperceptible, is free to roll her eyes
wherever she wishes. No matter what theories
they invent, she is before, outer, away, unending.
Still Luna.
More Luna.

I'd Give My Kingdom

I'd give my kingdom for a Clydesdale
Trotting down piano keys,
Destroy my dynasty for one last ride
In black and white golden ratio
Scales rounding

Away from bureaucratic battlefields,
Across capitalist plains,
Into the free-breathing sky—fly
Over the ocean's edge

Far from industrial design.
I'd shed this mortal coil, this limited shell
And like a naked nautilus, fling
Past the never-ending blue to colorless
Infinity, pure energy: nature
In its early rawness,
The gap of artistry between
Ice and fire's consummation.

I want to live
With all my senses
Expanded beyond small fingers
That blindly pick notes and pray.
Swirl my spirit around a galactic whirlpool
On the Painter's palette. Let me

Taste the salty stellar spray
Erupt from Cetus's blowhole,
Smell the damp celestial stalactites
Drip Milky Way sweat through iron beds,
See Triangulum's interwoven geometry
Pluck Lyra's harp strings,
Hear the deep bass *Om* of the central Be

Hum from too far to ever reach,
Feel the vibrations of dying stars
Pulse undulating patterns within me.

Oh yes, I'd destroy my dynasty
For a snippet of this eternal symphony.
Making a baby is an eighth note,
And missing it is merely a rest.
The orchestra blinks and moves on.
The melody remains intact,
The canvas colored Complete.

Prophetess

Cassandra divining at 7 years old:
I said I wanted 2 babies,
but when she hovered hands over my stomach,
closing eyes and speaking blessings,
I felt at my core it was a curse she laid.
Horrified, I wanted so badly to take it back,
believing it was real,
but I said nothing—
she looked so pleased with herself
and she was my only friend.

…double, double, cast out trouble…

I wrote spells on my bullies
and on myself
to undo the mind,
to undo the magic seen as good
with mouthfuls of vile.
I'd never heard of Shakespeare, yet I spake

…eye of newt and toe of frog, wool of bat and tongue of dog…

"Isolation prevents skin from touching.
No pregnancy if no one comes near.
Make them hate me, make them see
I am a divergent disease."
Ostracized, ostensibly, by myself.

…fire burn me; in cauldron I bubble…

Thank
Hecate
for sanctifying the witchcraft
of science and surgeries to assure

fertility remains a mere idea of make-believe.

And thank
Artemis
for bestowing her virgin blessing
as a barren womb, like a crop-free verdant tree
despite my later lack of chastity.

And even thank
Apollo
for ensuring my glowing independence and
that young prophetess
always disbelieved.

Wendy Pan

I can't have a child if I'm still a child.
I don't care how many years I've amassed,
I don't care how you record my time,
I don't care how you think I should be
wise and experienced.

I'm Wendy Darling
seeing her mother's eyes
when she looks in the mirror,
but it's her mother that still stares wistfully
at the second star to the right.

I'm Wendy, darling,
but this time I stayed in Neverland
playing pretend wife to Pan.
Pecked kisses and peach blushes:
perfcctly hot
enough to steep perfume from poppies;
in their red field we lie and sleep so soundly
after swallowing our gleeful shouts.

Reprimands nevermore. The Boys
know better than to call me Mother.
We left parents behind on purpose,
and in this Neverland,
we don't miss them at all.
It's exactly the paradise Peter promised,
our Saint Peter, devoted to the god Play.

There's plenty of food
ripe from the ground as perennial plants
and no poison grows
but from grown pirates' smoke.

Part of my fun is further education
and Peter does love his craftsmanship—

so we sing and we dance and we fight
(just for fun) and we laugh and we learn
and we build (just for fun) and we scream
and we run and we sleep (so much fun)

and the only frustration, the sole exasperation
comes when somebody stubs a toe.

I Kept the Stork Instead

The white stork brought me a picnic blanket,
four corners tied up nice and neatly.
I brandished my parasol like a baseball bat
(I couldn't own a bat),
ready to threaten him away,
but he bowed
and set the blanket down,
and it was strangely quiet for what I thought it was,
for what I had been taught it would inevitably be.

I loosened the knot with the sun-blocker's ferrule,
arm stretched out as far as it could go
to keep my body safely away

and what I saw inside
was

a picnic:

seared fish and flambéed frogs and
lightly-seasoned crabcakes and
hard-boiled eggs and a few fried grasshoppers...

and the stork remained bowed
like he didn't want to leave.

Long story short—

he dropped the baby he had been assigned
as soon as he took off.
Like a runaway child with a kerchief bundle,
he gathered up an offering to survive
unhindered by responsibilities,
and when he came,

he said,

"Adopt me instead."

So that is what I did.
I adopted my best friend.

He brandishes that beak
like a well-crafted dagger—
so much better than my flimsy parasol.
He plunges into my thick water
to eat my roe for supper.
He wraps me in devilish wings,
holding me close to his godly plumage
as he tells bedtime tales of pre-life flight.

By serene smiles, we preen,
snuggle, and savor sleep.

Of Banshees and Birthers

Daughter of Eve,
are you really so sad to find
a counterfeit among your ranks?
You have so many other sisters.
Leave me be to walk the path of Lilith
with the few cousins that do not share
in your commandment of descendants.
My freedom is no threat to you.
Lilith left, Eve arrived,
and each satisfied with their ending
of screams:
I, a banshee,
and you, a birther.

The Mom Moniker

My mind's eye sees how my life would be…
Liberty's kids erasing her name
and dressing her in Livery:
all she's addressed,
an anonymous label
of ewes high on oxytocin.

Happy in the chemical rush—
but no. No.
I won't be graffitied with the masses' title.
I'd rather grow wings, even if I crash
against gravity's reality.
Spread fingers wait for the lift,
free from the bars of others' bones.
No phalanges to fetter mine.
Wind in my face worth
the only screams I'll hear
from my own lungs, unsMothered.

Goes the Weasel

Monkeys run in circles to a 19th-century jig
played by an invisible orchestra.
When the music stops, the food is prepared.
They reach thumbs through set rings
to wrap hands around their select banana:
Human-granted names on labels sticky secure to the fruit.

Don't tell the monkeys I am the weasel.
I've always been the weasel
disguised as one of the troop,
waiting for my turn to wrap flimsy toes
over a simulated meal.

They don't see. Keepers lured us into cages
and locked the door behind our backs.
Those manipulators bred generations to believe
thirst is a myth told by doomsayers,
and the thirty bars that make each cage
are a comforting Mother's Embrace—
the right and only spot for sleep.
Food doesn't have to be worked for
beyond the dancing of smiling fools.

Every day, every damn day,
they reach out arms for bananas
in order to give birth to new slaves.

Weasels pop their heads up when disturbed and so
get popped on the ass to scurry back
into the wilderness. I feel the simians frown
at my risk of becoming
the morning buffet of an eagle eatery.
There aren't enough bananas. I don't want one and

I don't care. I'll take my chances
in the fresh air, feet quick and lungs deep.

A Sacred Feral

I never felt holier than when I defied holy men—
I spurned subservient prods by society's pricks
            to become
bare-teethed, brazen and bold, barking mad,
            Wild Again.
My naked feet are muddied in my own blood
mixed with seed-laden dirt by roots of living trees,
having spilled all weevil-infested progeny.
Together we stretch our leaf hands to the flaxen sun
in ecstasy of this soft moss freedom
away from the tyranny of Propriety.

Fencesitter

I wasn't always running wild
in green fields. I was raised
inside the white picket fence
with the *facts of life*:
- say grace before each meal
- elbows off the table
- speak when spoken to
- one day you'll be a mother

    here's a baby doll
    even though you're only three.
    learn early, prep your brain,
    for you were born
    with a uterine obligation,
    fertile ground for an accidental man
    (who could have been born like you
    but for chance) to fertilize, like a rose bush
    anchored to the ground, no way to run,
    and thorns, though sharp
    for semblance of defense,
    do not deter him.

I straddled
the fence for hours as a teen, hearing
- married sex is for procreation
- free sex is for God's damnation
- masturbation is abortion—murder; only men do

but the fence felt nice between my legs
and God was not even a whisper in the wind
to punish my pleasure. Then, I hopped off
on the wild side and ran, the wind in my hair,
and it felt even better.

Those circumscribed by the fence
who never learned to climb
called for my repentance, my regret
        -       running away only leads to loneliness
but I could barely hear them over my joyous laughter
and the walking trees welcomed me with open roots.

Chasm Eyes Span a Legion's Quest

My mind creates a black bridge above their words, linking
a skyscraper library, balconies balanced at cliff's edge,
to a stratospheric apple tree grove trickling diffused starlight.
The horde forms a fellowship to ford the gorge far below
and shout that I
shall
not
pass
through life unhindered by misery
of the miniature kind they brought upon themselves.
I don't even see them, rolling my eyes up to the heavens
they claim in screeches they represent.
They vilify me as *Babel Builder*,
but no deity has struck down the curlicues of my architecture;
no man has tried to confuse my tongue or deceive me,
save those gaslighters I tread above
on my wrought iron bridge among ravens in flight.

Among Sparrow Guano

A marked path,
pristine, sterile
dirt finally buries
all trash, litter,
mutated monkey bones.

Synthetic beauty
of art and architecture:
an acceptable loss
to bandage over ever-bleeding
deep human scars of
utility, efficacy, and convenience
that forever plagued the autotrophs.

The last artist loses himself
in fog, enfolding his essence
between ancestral trees.
He finds grandma pine,
hugs her
who hugs him back
as best she is able with sessile bark:
bittersweet pride
in the final descendant
of humankind
who spreads his seed

straight down into ground,
shrugging all the while.
If Gaia wants to gestate
photosynthetic demigods,
she can be a single mom.
Humans are done.

Spermatozoa among sparrow guano:
other creatures cannot tell the difference
and do not care.

Queen Loon of the Ruby Eye

My ruby eye stares down
the cormorant's green with envy
as she suns widened wings like a weak wall
across swamped stumps. Unlike her, I don't need
to stop and dry out after my submarine maneuvers.

I glide through the stream serene,
webbed feet making my own wake.
It ripples past my plumage. Right now,
I do not hunt, do not escape, do not journey.
I aim for aimless comfort. The warm sun on my beak

is the only friend I choose. I have a consort,
but we both know the best way to find fish
is to be the only feathered predator in our current.
No brood we've hatched. We live our own way,
happy accidents from eggs we didn't choose.

We visit when the sun kisses the water
from below, and again from above.
Our eyes meet, crowns touch. We repeat
the laughs we called across the acres.
I fly away once I've had enough of him

to the nest I made for myself by the shore,
with overgrown tree roots as my ceiling
and cool mud for my bed.
I close my eyes, and like a dove, I coo,
content with my companion of solitude.

"I am no more lonely than the loon in the pond that laughs so loud...."
Henry David Thoreau, *Walden* (1854)

Soft Moss Freedom

I lie naked on the bathroom floor
breathing
in through nose,
out through mouth
like blowing bubbles in my drink
with no etiquette to correct me.

A cotton towel cushions my bare bum
while warm steam from the Jacuzzi bath
coats my skin in mist and fogs
the mirror so I will not see the baby
crow's feet that have formed
around old eyes in a smooth face.

I keep them closed and imagine
a soft moss bed,
warm sun,
light mist of rain,
uninterrupted,
vulnerable

belly never curled to protect
delicate organs from jumping feet
and gripping fists.

My arms stretch wide to welcome
rainforest air
into lungs that are mine
alone.

Done

My maternal line
is full of unintended mothers
who had babies because
they were supposed to.
After two daughters, done.

My Nana almost got to
shelve her fertility
but for D-Day
and her sailor,
shell-shocked and sex-starved.
After one daughter, done.

My DNA is screaming
to not duplicate;
to live the life
she always wanted
now that I'm here
—and here is where it ends.
After no daughters
and no sons,
I rest, self-assured
and done.

I've Built a Nest

I've built a nest
in the eaves of this castle
for the comfort of me, myself,
and chosen guests.
I use its twigs for different things,
but not to host a hungry imp.
I have too much
to do, to oversee, to mutter
to invite another
that isn't even waiting
at the drawbridge.

Wild Comfort

I lay my eggs
over the side of the branch.
I watch as they fall to the ground
and break.
My nest is deep and warm.

Breakfast

You
say
my eggs
are fried? That's
exactly how my
husband likes them on the kitchen
counter before work:
slippery,
licked, dead
and
gone.

EVO

Extra virgin olive
sucked softly
by salivating mouths
puckering at the slightly sour salt

of seeds never grounded:
meant for oil, tongues, perching
on lips, nipples, inner thighs
as a tease

penetrating dreams,
no Teeth,

no threat
to a delicate future
waving finger fronds in wavering sunlight.

Pagan Nun

Just think of me as a pagan nun.
Sex rituals please my gods
who bless my willfully barren womb

with creative fingers
folding paper and words
into influence.

I've only been with one man.
Regardless of how much of the Kama Sutra's
erotic pages we've folded over,

strictly speaking, I'm chaste.
If the thought of Catholic nuns
summons a fleeting smile,

then smile at me.
Swallow the vomit coming
from the orgy you imagine.

Let Me

Let me live as a tortoise,
slow and steady in her pace.
She stops for sex when she wants,
and empties the eggs down a hole.

Lumbering on, no mind for the past,
she looks only at the horizon
seen by her own eyes, the only way
she can live any path at all.

Small smiles seen by those who care
to find, she loves rough dirt, tickles
of grass beneath large feet
knowing their way, never stumbling,

though onlookers think her gait uneven.

Mass Production

We've jammed
the assembly line of people
as two broken gears
longing to extend the tooth touch.
It's just not satisfying
flicking fangs like fingertips,
unlacing over and over
in service to the greater good's
never-ending supply.

From the beginning,
our obsolescence is planned: so
we willingly rust cogs
and stick
together at the altar of Mother Earth.
Our bodies unite in the prayer
murmured by machines' prey.

Tumbleweed Oasis

My uterus is a dusty Western town
tumbleweeds somersault through,
thistle hay knocked about to gather up
for pygmy butterflies' beds
and a world-weary Drifter's cot.

Stinging sandstorms would rub
baby skin bloody raw,
but rough and weathered leather
lives to face my Dust Bowl,
and he licks the porcelain clean.

I hide my groundwater well,
but for him the drip echoes
around the saloon's broken glass,
even late mornings
when the sun has burned off the wind.

He drinks his fill and lies to other squatters
so he may keep the rare liquid, like gold,
all to himself. This Oklahoma ghost town
quenches a curious mind
yearning to explore in private.

Busybody society is behind him,
bustling on the coast, building up
crowded cities that trash their hours
living by duty like captive cattle:
buy, breed, and feed.

Mud Bath

There's no water at the bottom of my well.
I'm full of happy
chemicals stoppering the flow
of a natural spring that washed away
my bedrock my birthday.
High tide groundwater weighed me down
and suffocated sand that needed air
to slide across the core of my dried apple world.

Plants wither when planted on my planet.
I hold no minerals and let in no
photo for synthesis. But this darkness is safety
for secret meetings in midnight blue
away from staring cameras poking paparazzi
fingers. Welling eyes, bruised, they delight in—

never here. Not this deep, where only he
spelunks naked for the mud bath of his life.
He takes his rope and rappels down my slick sides
'til his dusty work boots squelch sour cherry soil.

X *Still Marks the Spot*

I can't believe
butter
flies from my barren cave
instead of bats:
a drizzle of liquid scales, chitin
like lemon zest, damp dust
to rest alongside the pollen on my tires
for no one to know. Which smell,
which muscle spasm causes men
to sneeze? Butter onto butterflies....

Caterpillars of wide girth
wear lemon peel wings
split evenly in a single, fluid cut
around the circumference—
a blood eagle without the violence.
I cried out, but then, so did he.

Our moans earn no warriors' rest.
But Freyja is pleased and welcomes us
to her lush lovers' paradise

when my own wings rain gold
eagles on a horde of sovereigns
and disappear in the rising sun.

Tempting

Pando, he cloned himself
quaking aspen pickets to form
a natural fence in Fishlake Forest.

Under his asexual ancestral grove,
our arms prickle and flush
under the leaf-trickled light
tickling your eyes.

Second thoughts might get us caught.
Hesitation wastes time. In this moment,
the only ones who eye us
are the deer doing the same.

Everyone ran to the coast, scantily clad.
Rid yourself of all claddings, my darling,
and my soft curves shall decorate your chest
like delicately peeling lichen on the trunk
I shove you against.

I'm ready to kiss. Let's do this right
now, for the rites of spring
are almost ended.
Don't be shy.
Come
for pleasure alone.

Chosen Skins

Feeling safe at last with my spouse
Away from blood bonds I never asked for,
Malaise of the past I leave behind.
Ice-cold cells surf my brainwaves for those
Loved ones that neglected and abused me,
Yet melt at the touch of chosen skins.

My Undivided Attention

Dear Husband,

You can have the honor
of my constant eyes, hands
that cradle your arms, hips
that hold all your legs

and no energy vampire
reaches pinching fingers
through my cervix
to drain our shared sex drive

and no sanguine dragon
scratches soiled talons
against my labia
to steal our treasured time

and no fairy changeling
schemes some tricksy screaming
by my ankles
to halt our loving life.

I will never have your babies
suckling the estrogen I saved
for your balance. Forever,
my priority is your pleasure.

One Winter's Night

Your wiry brunette beard grew through faded lipstick stains.
I dare to color the hairs in rouge all over again.
You cringe to be left makeup-marked, but I know you
love the attention. My bare legs rub against your boxers.
You can't lie
                    there,
not after your tongue starts licking my lobe.

Five layers of soft blankets guard your truth
only I may witness. I trace my palms
across fingernail marks fading on your blue-collar back,
and I snuggle closer, wiggling between laughs
like a cat preparing
                    to pounce
a mischievous mouse.

Smooth chest against smooth chest:
motor oil would slide right off
our saltwater-taffy fins, stuck together,
all tacky without any wrappings left in the box.
This sailing ship needs no motor
                    nor a captain
so far north in latitudes uncharted.

The ocean under a starry sky is cracked glass
but for our wake. The water laps softly,
matching tempo with flesh percussion.
Lucky black cat wanders in when we are done
and curls against
                    my flat belly
(no matter how fat from food).

Last summer's sable fur blankets the white keys
of my ancestor's piano back home, save

the lowest note. I've memorized the tone;
I press it in my throat to mimic
your seductive, demonic growl—what strains
                 that pain me to reach
make you a part of me.

So What if I Die Alone?

I'll be an old biddy with no one left to love,
headbanging a stiff neck to sentimental heavy metal
until vertigo constructs a tilt-a-whirl pendulum fusion
in my carnival brain, and I spin out onto the floor.
My heart stops in shock, but my smile remains. In my winter,
I never had to concede to someone else's taste.

My cats will kiss my lips before the first bite of my flesh
like a strange Snow White twist,
yet my expression will be peaceful in its eternal sleep
because I lived the life I wanted
—sterile and feral—
and I couldn't care less what happens to my body
once I'm no longer inside.

The Meaning of Life

The meaning of my life
is more than a biological imperative,
goes beyond the physical
into the spiritual, the imaginative, the Great
Intelligence binding us all together
as neurons of one mind.
Too many is insanity.
Too few loses function.
Enough is carried over, now
that mine can carry out its code
until that allotted time
the synapse fizzles out
and a new directive steps forward
from another's production.

The meaning of my life
is to be lived in this very moment.
I'm meant to exist by virtue of existing
and when I die, I'm dead. That's that.

Recipe for a Childless Cat Lady

- One bolt cutter
- Two stale raisins
- A handful of sunflower seeds, or more depending on how many times you've had sex
- A pool OR a car OR an orchard basket
- Tumbleweed
- Three boxes of condoms for the whore OR nothing at all since she's so ugly no one would fuck her
- Two breasts (one will suffice in a pinch, and they don't have to be the same size)
- A dead tree trunk that was felled before it grew any branches
- At least one cat (add to taste—the more cats, the more authentic the dish)
- A dash of misery to validate the jealous commentary of conservative politicians

Keep the bolt cutter handy throughout the preparation.

Place the raisins on the kitchen counter, or the floor if you don't have a finished kitchen. Renovations are hard without a man. Obviously, if you're childless, you're also single. Married women are heterosexual and have babies.

Take the bolt cutter by the handles and press each raisin with the jaws. Take the flattened fruit, and what little juice is left, and shove them up your tired vagina to replace the long-dried pomegranate arils inside you.

Eat the sunflower seeds, one at a time. Eat one for every sexual experience you have had, and name them all. They could have been babies.

Walk outside. Empty the pool of water, or take the engine out of the car, or remove the fruit from the basket. Place the tumbleweed in the empty container. Know that this is you. Know that no one would use you in this condition. Know that your only value is your usefulness to others. Know that a man is the water, the engine, the fruit, and is valuable himself without the holding.

Go inside. Wait for the sun to hide its face from your nasty proclivities. Place the condoms on your nightstand and call yourself a murderess. Fondle your breasts and realize it feels good because your hands are meant to be suckling infants.

Look out the window at the prone tree trunk. It's dead in the dusk. It never grew to raise hands up to the Father. Dead, dead, dead, just like you. It…squirrel?

Watch the squirrel hop in and out of the trunk, hiding acorns for future food. Watch her chase off the others. Watch her grow comfortably chubby in her contentedness.

Take the bolt cutter and sever the chain around your ankles. Rip the label of "Ball" from your shirt. Call your cats. Feel them purr against your legs. Forget this recipe.

Remember the test that told you to read all of the instructions before beginning. At the end, it'd say, "Put down your pen and sit quietly, ignoring all of the questions that came before." You fell for that as a child. You'd stand up and put your thumb to your temple, fingers raised in the shape of a naïve question to those you thought knew better than you, and you'd say, "I'm Bullwinkle Moose," just like the paper told you to do. And a few others would do it too. You'd look around at classmates sitting quietly and wonder, why weren't they following the rules? Wasn't it their duty to obey those in power? Didn't they want a good grade, and praise? In your strive to succeed, you failed. In your

need to fit in, be obedient, have a perfect day, you made yourself
into a fool.

Hold that dash of misery in your hands, study it, laugh at it, and
squash it between your palms. Take a deep breath. And another.
And another. Enjoy the silence.

Safe and Protected

They Never Told Me I'd Be Screwed

When I was a child,
they never told me
I had a uterus
and my eggs were more valuable than
I.

They never told me
my penis'd peers
were the ones who could be
whatever.

I wanted to live
free
my mind.

They never told me
the organ-
ization I never asked for
would follow me through life,
a cult meting out curses
for an unful-
filled prophecy.

They never told me,
and that was their mistake.
When I saw the demographics
on the intake form of Life—
Ha! I tore the Script into pieces
and threw their hopes onto a fire
of My Own design.

Because I *will* be
whatever
I want.

I Defoliate

Minute minds gaze at their navels and crave
new skin, peach fuzz and pits to raze
Venus flytraps in the stroller-strewn delta.
Deadly nightshade blooms in tandem
with their rusted chain-choked cycles.
But me, my rhythm is full, flush, and flowing.

My immune system waits
at the watchtower, with Agent Orange
to rain down on the raiding rider
embryo; mustard-gas canisters
at the ready against
a camouflaged marauder

—all the white cells see
(no Light exists to refract).
Immunity attacks invaders:
what would aim flaming grenades
at the base of my beech castle,
tendrils climbing like wolfish wisteria at sunset.

I don't need to lower the drawbridge,
I don't need to lift the gates,
I don't need to order fanfare
for a pineapple to my endometrium.
Guarded I will remain
by bone soldiers and plasma shields.

Flush

I don't own a turkey baster.
I have no need for one
when a ladle pours his white sauce
down a different drain.
It drips through the garbage disposal
soaking old tomato slime,
loose broccoli buds,
and rotten deviled eggs
I couldn't stomach to finish
at Sunday brunch.
Full-blast faucet and lavender Fabuloso
flushes that shit out to a treatment plant
to be chemically neutralized.
No maggots will live in my house.
No parasites will make their way
from dirty hands to my gut.

Go Bite a Wire

June 24, 2022

I watched a bird bite a power line
and I thought that might be a good idea
today when my death was ordained
by the hands of ham-fisted men.
If I'm to die, at least I'll keep control
in my own delicate finger
sandwiches they think I make
for their calloused tongues.

Watch them all fall to my electric taste
when my apron's covered in tomato paste.

Find Me a Eunuch

June 24, 2022

They've taken away the doctors
They've taken away the doctors
They've taken away the doctors
They've put their faith
in the strings of my heart
formed to beat too fast
if it works to create another;
my life sacrificial, acceptable
to make vulnerable food for their feast.

They've taken away the surgeons
They've taken away the surgeons
They've taken away the surgeons
They've put their faith
in old blind women, and talk, and hips
not wide enough to pass developed brains,
and lies that we've always lived to be pregnant,
every perineum made to split
and snap back like Velcro.

They've taken away the nurses
They've taken away the nurses
They've taken away the nurses
They've put their faith
in a god that didn't create us
bipedal, to push out unfinished
crawling mewling on all fours
crying for death when no hands
are there to touch us.

They've taken away the condoms
They've taken away the condoms
They've taken away the condoms

They've put their faith
in our *naughty* nature,
a lack of chastity to yield flesh
to abuse the only breathable planet.
They say it's meant for
us (no:
men) to take over.
A human godhood,
a humble pride
that cannot answer
why food must first breathe.

Who cares to care for wom—
the flesh laboratories
temperature
controlled to curate
more of the same minds?

Find me a eunuch to love
Find me a eunuch to love
Find me a eunuch to love

(I Will Be) No Host

Tended to grow to fullest fate:
A fruit intended for genuine use.
Siblings were cultivated to create.

Plump, juicy tang of nightshade,
Once left to my own device, the only abuse
As tended, I grow to fullest fate.

My former flower had a mate
But this stamen has faded to refuse,
For only siblings were cultivated to create.

Not I—and now it shall be too late.
These germs will not throw a noose
Over a life tended to grow to fullest fate.

Green has no room to gestate
When a knife halts the path to reproduce.
I say, my siblings were cultivated to create.

Me, I am I, the one made to captivate
Papillae of tongue, yet remain obtuse,
For I was tended to grow to fullest fate,
while siblings were cultivated to create.

A Great Fall

they Humped Her mercilessly,
Dumping cum into Her yolk.
then they waited for the shell to harden,
but She threw Herself from the wall.

all the king's horses skid
on spilled albumen, and all the king's men
cracked their skulls on sandstone bricks.
Humpty Dumpty became just a dashed egg
to their bayonet whims

and the mouth piece smiles to know
shell shards serve little protection
for rapacious boys.

She gathers their broken bones
and bathes them in the whites
that cooked on hot pavement,
molding armor to hold Her spirit.
they tried to fix Her.
now they're dead
and She endures,
the leader's tibia Her herculean club.

Autonomous

She ends the reign before it begins,
aiming an arrow from Diana's quiver.
Cold wood against small lips, large
promises to herself to complete
the circumference 'round forests
undisturbed by roots men ripped
to pave Roman roads through glades
no one invited them to tread.

The arrow trembles in her grasp.
She fights to keep hold in spite
of baritone clouds closing in
across the empty orb to muddy it
with purple tones of scream and suffering.

Her body's blood on her hands is better
than teeth and skin and hair within,
outside-in like some inverted cannibal
stealing life from her own roots, ripped
without permission
instead of leaves plucked from above: still
without permission
but something she could
spot,
seize,
skirmish

to shield
her being,
knowing her enemy on sight.
She preserves anonymous flight after the fight
is won. No legacy for larcenists of lust.

I'll Forage the Pavement of Back Alleys

I'll paint blue berries over my belly.
Cohosh will hush haunting howls
long before lungs develop. Then,
Pennyroyal will rise like Pennywise,
stalk from flower, and again,
ladderlike from storm drains to the sky.
The petals play itsy bitsy spider,

venomous to the organ playing host.
The invitation was never supposed to go out
and I never welcomed this party.
I shall make a tincture
with marjoram, mugwort, yarrow
and settle in for a nap
during the ensuing storm,
cozy in my chrysalis.

God, you cursed us with wombs.
But you gave us these plants too,
then, through the men you had us make,
forbade us to learn
how to read
books on botany
and warning labels.
We learned anyway.

Adam let Lilith fly away and left
Eve to wander the garden:
it seems your man doesn't quite care
what I do with this form
once he's had his fun with it.

Watch me unmake the fate
I didn't freely will.

Manifest

All I did was pick a weed
but you treat me like dandelions
are 14-carat-gold conquistadors,
like simpering Cortés is the sun
of all sons, Quetzalcoatl—
you'd have me believe it was precious
Destiny, despite his precocious invasion
into green land that never needed him,
no! that dried to yellow drought
for his persistent presence,
choking life right out of its roots.
            My roots
are preserved by the lion's uprooting.

Streamers

A fine blade slices a piece of my meat
I don't need or feel.
Forceps grasp and detach
Smartly, as a steam clean sucks out old vomit stains.
I beg to see the proof.
"Stitch it in my back," I say.
"Slit the tubes and let the fallopes fly
As wings outside the skin."
I want *that party*,
Already disgusted with my decision,
To viscerally witness what the invisible incisions

Left behind.
I'm liberated.

Let them see
I hired a demolition crew
To destroy the bridge between factory and fertile field,
So the steel pylons and cable stays
Recycle me
Into a prudent Icarus
Pedaling a da Vinci flying machine.
Silk membranes in moonlight above pristine pine moss—
Reclusive heron
Refusing cousin stork's offer of work.

Presence of Mind

I'm a classy wild woman,
elitist and cultured but never tamed,
feminine but not fully female.
I took the storage out of my
eggshell
exterior: simply a polished mirror
to the empty souls that gaze
only at my posterior
curves that belie my lack
of childbearing capacity.

I love to be that liar
seducing eyes
for no finality,

for no presents
from their intentions,
for no presence
outside their delusions.

Assigned Female Glamour

Self-inflicted sterile, so
my beauty is just a fairy glamour.
I feel safer.

Stranger,
I will *never* bear your tainted legacy
no matter how firm you insistently

thrust. Assail me with your crooked mast.
Breach my jetty. I may crumble and bleed
but I will not die by your parasitic hand
in all the days to come.
My pier too slippery for baby barnacles to suction.

Agender angel triumphant
wades with chin held high,
tunic flowing in the tide.

Spayed

I fixed me—
cured my fecundity
right in front of your face
as you screamed
that the vaccine was poison
drying me out.
Good sir, I pray to your god
you honestly believe your words.

I fixed me—
blessed my body with sterility
so your seeds fail to sprout
no matter how savagely you scatter
and shove into my soil.

I fixed me—
de-stressed my accidental mammal.
Pardon my emancipation
from your expectations.
I donate my living cadaver
to his research alone;
my priority his delighted discovery
and no parasite will prevail.

Grand Jeté

They say I must become one with the hive—
But by joining their side, I will soon die
So I leap from cradle to casket to stay alive.

Reproducing genes the only means to survive:
Transferring life to larvae, yet cicadas don't cry—
They say I must become one with the hive.

My thorax has a use, but it's never to thrive,
Feeding vines bleeding tree and carcass dry;
So I leap from cradle to casket to stay alive.

The mother-mind is the de rigueur dive
Into a sacrificial pit with a blissful sigh.
They say I must become one with the hive.

But every inhale of mine is a chance to revive,
And these still-spry wings would rather fly,
So I leap from cradle to casket to stay alive.

Nonexistent kids I selfishly deprive
of my single ashen piece of maple syrup pie.
They say I must become one with the hive.
No—I leap from cradle to casket to stay alive.

After Life / Comes Death

I don't mind plants growing from my corpse.
That's fine.
But I don't need life bursting out of me
Before I die
Accelerating my demise.

I don't mind the cycle
Life—Death—Life
But I don't need life overlapping
To share same flesh, blood, bone,
Breath I thought was all mine.

I'll hold tight to my one of a kind
Until crows wipe their beaks
in my hollowed eyes
and red-shouldered hawks dance
my leaf-tangled sinew
across Shenandoah sunshine.

Ready With Retorts

A Child Named Inner

Ah…yes, of course I have a child.
I did my duty
and nurtured the daughter
I was.
What?
I said, I was
the fertile mother you expect.
I matured in thought and feeling
to heal my child
named Inner. She is quite healthy now.
So sickly when she was small.
Do you want to see a picture of
~~me when I was three~~
I mean, her?
Let me tell you all about my girl
inside.

Her favorite food is cheddar cheese,
favorite composer is Tchaikovsky,
favorite animal is Big Bird—a canary
(but she loves him specifically
because he's so tall, so we agree
he's a pollen-dusted cassowary).

Hey, come back!
I should have known.
You only care that I used my body
for its requisite pain.
You wanted to hear I screamed
that ear-splitting women's salvation,
but her little voice in the real world
is irrelevant. Whether I had a baby,
you care, but not for who she is.
Just another wet cog in your machine.

No Kids, No Future

I remember when *I* was your future.
Now I'm just
a sow of sour milk,
a broodmare,
a breeding cow
to be put out to pasture if I don't comply
with the unattended bulls' vicious rut

to give the green grass a new calf
trampling, gnashing, ripping
until dust is all that remains
of our beautiful world

but hey,
at least the species lasted
long enough
to kill all the rest
with our hemlock tongues.

A Heifer? Yes

If we're treating women like livestock
(since they're "females" only
worth their wombs)
then fine. I'm a heifer.
Now go away.

No? Ugh. Listen,
a heifer is a future cow—
she's not given birth yet.
Except I've changed *yet* to *ever*.
Call me what you will.

A man's hand pets my spine
and I even let him ride me
but that hand will never
brand a bulbous belly.
He feels no need to brag:

> "Look at my prize!
> Look what I did to her—
> I control her forever now
> as the mother of my calf.
> I own her meat and eat it too."

He's a renegade, not a cowpoke,
and we ride wild together, in a frenzy
away from the auction where
other heifers line obediently up,
cheering to get pumped.

So I'm worthless?
Good. Now go away.

I Did Not Consent to Motherhood

I did not ask to be born.

I did not ask to be born with a uterus.

I did not ask to be born with a uterus
that politicians think they can control.

I did not ask to be born with a uterus
that politicians think they can control
by telling me I should just stay chaste.

I did not ask to be born with a uterus
that politicians think they can control
by telling me I should just stay chaste,
then accusing me of undocumented abortions.

I did not ask to be born with a uterus
that politicians think they can control
by telling me I should just stay chaste,
then accusing me of undocumented abortions
because women are not safe.

I did not ask to be born with a uterus
that politicians think they can control
by telling me I should just stay chaste,
then accusing me of undocumented abortions
because women are not safe
in their bedrooms until breastfeeding babies.

Quiet Desperation

"You don't want kids?
You're selfish; you hate them!"

hatred has no place here
I desperately need you to understand
it's not even about the wanting
I feel it deep in my blood and bones
that I'm full as I am
and pregnancy would be parasitic

it's not selfish
to live the life meant for me
and honor the life
you made for you,
that you were called to and
felt instinctual to you

my instinct says no

please
let it be
me for me
you for you

A Place

My lack of kids gives yours a place
and the chance to breathe cleaner air
in a paradise of waning waste.
My lack of kids gives yours a place
to find a job with no rat race
or waiting list for prime daycare.
My lack of kids gives yours a place
and the chance to breathe cleaner air.

In The Closet

It was nice in the dark with fabric softener
filling my breath and the quiet with snuggles,
self-soothing like my momma taught me
when I'd scream for company. I learned
to love the silken dark both warm and cold
because it was safe and never confronted my comfort

with expectations. But I was left without a choice.
Once I came of age, I was yanked out
of my lovely closet and thrown onto the street.
Little layover in the bed and couch.
Right on the pavement, made to run
with the sun in my eyes but no blessing
of damaged retinas restoring the dark.
I turned away over and over,
screaming again and again, *No!*
but the earth rotates.

My voice remained. I always said no.
Every day the sun would rise and pester me
with intrusive questions. *No. I won't.*
Melt my clothes off my back and say
it's the natural way. Bury me in the soil
to keep me from running.
I will still say *uh-uh* without a tongue,
for I will die
before the darkness is never returned
by the night, my lovely, beautiful night.

A thousand suns I can face
as long as they set once more
and leave me to my delicious lonesome.

You Can't Know Until You Do It

Mama Bear asks how we can know
childfree is the way to be
for ourselves
without
experiencing what would be
our children,
but it's not bleu cheese, Mrs. Bear.

I can't gag and tell the waiter to take it back.
The waiter would just laugh
and say "you made your choice,
now choke and keep quiet about it."

Mrs. Bear would like to be our waiter.

But I've picked a different restaurant
with fine china and no need
for locks on glass cabinets.
Teacups rest on saucers upon doilies
and top shelf liquor lies within arm's reach
for those who prefer their tea
Long Island Iced.

I know I'd hate sewage in my water
without having tried it.
It's not even on the menu.
The proprietors know us well.

I know I'd hate fraying wool
fibers stabbing my thighs like cacti
behind my sheer silk skirt.
Their seats are muslin on bamboo.

I know I'd hate contracting
flesh-eating disease,
consuming me so I can't consume.
Knives are sheathed in folded napkins.

I know I'd hate cockroaches
crawling across my plate and
tarantulas dropping on my red pumps.
The busboy swipes finished dishes.

I know I'd hate the pain
of a copperhead bite
right before it killed me.
The manager keeps the building cold.

I know I'd hate drowning:
waterboarded to the point of nearly dying
from shock and hypoxia.
Water is served in Irish coffee mugs.

I know I'd hate falling off a cliff
to break my back body-slamming
the crashing waves or jagged rocks,
but Mama Bear, if you honestly believe

you can't know
until you do it,

please, do it.

Rot

Amy says kids are *pure happiness*
And those who don't have them
Are poor, but—

Who is poorer?
The woman with no apples
Or the woman with a spoiled one?
The woman with no orchard to her name
Or the woman with a blight?

Propaganda only works on those
Who don't understand
Paradise is overrun with parasites
On Earth. Babylon's hanging gardens were
Destroyed by war despite meticulous pruning.

Freedom is its own wealth.
Honey, I'm content
With no Eden to keep me grounded
And as minimal rot as I can manage.

Spoke in the Wheel

Be a good girl.
Show
that you conform.
Prove
you are not a threat.
Obey
society's rules.
Know
your place.
Enjoy
raising up boys.

Don't dare defy
even one rule, we cannot tell
how many more you might
spasmodically splinter
in our (up)tight-knit hub
to divide the wheel
from the planned path
you had no say in paving.

A minor deviation
deserves ostracization.

Dear Tradwife

"Modesty.
Service.
Submission.
Motherhood.
A Godly Woman
knows her place
and fulfills her role with a smile."

Oh shut up, you milk thistle.

Viceroy butterflies hover.
Your flower owns such dainty petals
choking the life from unassuming thyme.
Six thousand seeds spread
to form dense populations

no better than a wildfire,
feeding its offspring on the backs of brush.

Your spine-edged cheekbones cut
like the jagged glass rim
of a floor-shattered jar.
Preserved onions exposed—
one lick would poison your Papillion.

You think you add classic flavor
if people would just prepare properly
with modest caution, but most cry,
raging at sulfuric cuts.

Criticism makes you double down,
saying, "Why yes, I am," while twisting
words like a unicorn lollipop dyed red.
You take another moniker for vanity.

"Holy thistle, blessed milk
made by God through Adam,
meant to heal man and harm livestock.
Who cares about minor minds
destined for our dinner table?"

Calling yourself holy
doesn't make you blessed.

Cows produce milk for their babies,
yet gaze at me with understanding eyes:
higher lifeforms by far than you
spitting into the mouths of your own
to spread a Wordy disease.

Antidote for alcoholics who need to settle
self-destructive ways, I'll admit,
and good for you keeping men grounded,
but this world has many roads.
Your unpaved country path
does not cure me, no; the bumps bloat me
like a blimp until I spew ballast on my shoes.

You can be happy with your decision
without thinking everyone should make it.

Just like men,
your genitalia are not all you're good for,
and mine are good for nothing
filled with rotten yolk by decayed stems.

Dead Branch

You i.d. me as a dead branch on my family tree
but I'm still attached to the ancestral rings.
At night I sway in the same breeze.
I scrape the window of your broken glass god,
the one you say planted our seed,
and I taunt him with the primordial mother
buried beneath his NPD.
He suffocated her silent until
any mention of the -dess is heresy
but her spirit thrives on the wind
wrapping 'round my bark, carefree,
dead but breathing in feeling
happy to be hugged. I host a hive of bees.

But one day, your broken glass god
will get sick of seeing our tree
fat outside his door, our swollen trunk
obscuring his view of the valley
and he will summon an axe
and he will sharpen it on his teeth
and he will slam the front door
and he will chop history to debris
in one hit. The heartwood bleeds
for his beloved sun's kindling
as he swallows my queen's honey.

For My Christian Sisters

Jesus was blessed without offspring
and *be fruitful* was never His command.
Why do only childless men get to sing
Jesus was blessed without offspring?
Barren Christians follow a red-letter king.
From birth, baby girls' lives are baby-planned,
but Jesus was blessed without offspring
and *be fruitful* was never His command.

Different Kind of Fun

"You're a pool with no water."

So I'm a skate park
Doling out bruises but nobody's drowning
And I'm enjoyed all year 'round.

Empty Barrel

"You are like an empty barrel."

Yep.
A barrel is made
with the possibility to store things,
but it doesn't automatically do so.

A barrel is content
being a barrel
and doesn't feel it lacks a purpose.

Only the person who wants to use it
and can't open it
calls it useless,
but that only means
it's useless to that person,

and it doesn't care.
It doesn't define itself
based on its usefulness to others.
It exists regardless,
and takes up space
whether you like it or not.

Oh, and a barrel
is an inanimate object
made of lifeless wood,
so let's not reduce people
to dead matter.

Disaster Artist

I was told
I don't have my life together
because I haven't made
a new human
in my baby factory.

As though
the baby factory
is my entire campus
and not just
some dilapidated corner lot
that may or may not
be bulldozed in the near future,
a small blemish among
seventy-seven other
magnificent baroque abodes.

My life is breathing,
my life is eating,
my life is p(l)aying,
my life is shelter,
my life is art,
my life is one
hundred percent ordered
together exactly as I want it
without the chaotic graffiti
a kid with a crayon
would vandalize
across all my buildings.

But please, by all means,
go ahead and paint over me
colors of mess and misery
to justify your own disappointments.

Pilot

I make my own meaning
by choosing my care
carefully
outside myself,
flying zigzags from cloud to tree to cloud,

not auto-piloting empathy
straight up to the son,
vertically free-falling back to land
always at my brood's private nest,
directed by the same old men
of my grandfather's ground control.

Stolen Eggs

Magnolia seed pods are cocoons
for infant fairies. She discovered
their petrified heads in stasis
sticking out the small grenades.
Collected carefully, she kept them
warm in maple leaf beds, hoping
to see them hatch one day, but no
way to know how long to incubate.
She thought this was practice
for motherhood—just set them up
and let them be what they would be.
Nurturing was ensuring they were snug,

nothing more. Laying eggs is easy.
But that's not what mammals do,
and neglecting eggs gets them stolen.

Little girl, don't let the fairies find you.
Angry ovulators think themselves mothers
before the chore even begins, and curse
thieves to suffer, more than others. In blood.

Like mantises, these feathered predators
gather up their precious eggs and pray
spontaneous conception on you,
suddenly their immature enemy.
She wants to know what it is like?
Her people urge her to practice?
She will, now. Her fathers won't stop it.

They don't need to find you.
Devilish thoughts fly a southern current
and name you a distorted Maria.

You whimper to deaf air,
"The egg stays within? Bouncing
against my tender organs with no pipe
to release the melody? But where...
where does it go once it hatches?"

The fairies smile deviously.
There is a tunnel, but they've sealed it.
A knife's your only way out of this.
A knife sawing your most vulnerable softness
that quadrupeds curl in a circle
to guard. Little girls tied to a wishing well,
unable to reach even a penny-thought
to the stale pool below, only long for
escape. Just two feet to the cave next door,
where water falls and water breaks
and there's no trace of accidental sins.

But in chains, little girls can't hide
from the grow(l)ing inside.

Inhabit

The blue jay on my shoulder
drowns out other people's speech.
I can't stand to hear their cries
of supplication, obligation, expectation—
they all try to enslave me in frustration.
But I have always been free
despite the claims on my spirit
and my body's imprisonment on this one planet
that sustains my incarnation. Always free.
Free to fly, free to lie, free to sigh, free to die
from the moment I first inhaled cut off from the umbilical
that grew me as a new organ of my mother, then mutated
into a true sexually transmitted Human Disease.
The blue jay squawks again and I wish
there was a way to shed this body and know
I could still see, breathe,
inhabit this bird and fly so far
from the crushing oppression
that blackens the feathers of hope
and singes my eyes.

Alone A Threat

On a streetlight he sits, quietly contemplating
the sunlight stream from morning cloud,
when three bats with venomous fangs bare

C
      R
A
      S
H

down from the blue to wound his black head.
Back up, zigzag flight pattern, down
to his scratched scalp again. He flinches, ducks,
but their aim is true. And they don't stop. They don't stop
for him to see they are smaller birds. They don't stop
to tell him they would prefer he not eat the babies
he doesn't know exist. They don't stop mocking
bird to bird of prey that he, alone, is Danger.

Minding his own life, staring at the sun.
Danger with a capital D.
Their offspring more valuable
for being more numerous.
How dare his presence even begin
to threaten their immortality?

Vulture

You swerve at me and say that I'm crazy.
I deserve my wrinkled bald head
flattened under tires
rather than withstanding more acid
from the intestines you claim I swallow
bathing in gore.
Since I won't lay an egg,
obviously I crave the complete opposite
of birth, like life doesn't flow before a death.
No new breath from my cloaca
means I want all breathing to cease.

I don't understand how you think—
and you don't understand how
I continue on
like my barren Egyptian sisters,
spontaneously born from the air—
so I am named Insane.

Please Stop, It's a Person

I don't understand the obsession you have
with other women's babies. It's not yours.
Why are you clambering to get your claws on it
and smell it and wipe your crusty lips on its head?
It's a person, not a toy or piece of cake.

Reproductive hormones must flood the brain
and make you want to shove the infant's head
back up your own vagina so you can push it out
yourself and grow your brood
like geese that steal goslings from other flocks.

That, or literally eat it
for prolonged youth, or prenatal nutrition.
Not a far cry from eating the placenta.
Reality is stranger than fiction.
When did cannibalism stop surprising me?

I'll Catch Your Stones

I hold no infants in my arms.
Throw your stones.
Empty hands can catch them
and throw the bloody rocks right back.
You still can't believe
I'll take my chances with my own
pursuit of happiness?
Don't be surprised
at the lake of spit in your grave.

Five

Five years old:
the only girl in class
who'd kissed a boy,
imagined a prince's love...

Grade five:
the only girl who didn't know
how sex worked,
permission slip denied.

Ten and five:
all kisses left behind;
no boy wanted to teach
the sheltered girl more.

Four times five:
let me tell you how sweet
missionary can be, finally
learned from the Internet.

Five, five times:
all caught up with fingers,
I laugh at demands for babies
from those who told me no.

Disembodied Words

Disembodied words dance
around my eyes in no particular order
anymore. The same questions ad nauseum
bore to tears unless I pick them apart
and play with the order like a chaotic child
forcing puzzle pieces together by biting
off the edges. I dance around the outskirts
anyway. They treat me like a child-
bearing child anyway. They want that,
they've said so. They don't hide it,
yet I'm the freak. Okay. Anyway…

    different   your own
Who   will take   care?
        You'll regret childbirth.
The human race will mind when you're old.
        Don't you want to die out?
It's different when your family name is a real woman.
        But you'd make such a good cancer.
You will never know your biological clock.
        Aren't you curious to cure your mind?
You forget the pain of what they'll look like.
        It's worth regret later.
You aren't a future husband.
        Don't you like human nature?
Real parents make their own grandchildren.
        True love is ticking.
If you wait until you have kids, you'll never have money.
        The only reason to get married is selfish.
What if you never parent?
        You'll change your parents' kids.
Don't have children if you're an adult.

I caught their words
and flicked them around in the air
and now they sound like funny
music to my ears.

Pour Little Teapot

I'll be a little teapot
For my gentleman.
I'll let him hold my handle,
Lay his mouth right on my spout.

But strangers who think
They can crash into our kitchen?
Men who think
To slam my ceramic and burn my base
To punish me
For the little milliliter
Of water I'm able to hold?

I'll never steam for them.
And if they touch me while I am,
I'll be burning them back.
When they tip me over,
I'll pour acid out.

Hen

Without a rooster,
eggs are just breakfast
for a hungry mammal.
Ovulation doesn't make
a hen a mother, and this
doesn't make her less of a hen.
She is one hundred percent whole
chicken, the same flavor
as her squawking friends.

Briar Ratio

They don't seem to understand
my eggs are full of briars

despite the youthful bloom
still glowing upon my cheek.
I've always held briars within

ever since the first boy betrayed me
and I knew my life would be full
of fights faced alone
no matter whose hand was held.
Only I can inhabit this mind.

No other soul can enter here
and no other body can hold me.
If the briars grow, nobody else can
feel the pain of the thorns' stab
piercing my liver. So nobody minds. They say
I can live with a portion of poor health.
I'm a woman, after all.
Well—I'm something else entirely.

Lesser Creature

Like a tree grown for lumber,
you don't care if my leaves rot,
if woodpeckers drill me a thousand holes,
if lichen and moss destroy my roots—
as long as my trunk swells thick with water,
and enough light stimulates my juices.

The shade I cast on lesser creatures
is just a band-aid, ripped off before the bleeding stops,
and you laugh at the fur on fire,
blistering boils on vulnerable victim's skin.

As long as the man-
ufactured structures remain erect,
my ass is grass
dead and yellowed, burned to decompose in leveled dirt
so that the children you force into existence
can't identify the color green.

I am every woman
and every woman is Mary:
worthless without a womb,
craving pain for a potential Christ

so someday a son might touch the sun in a victory pose
after he frames the stained-glass window of a mega church
with my stripped wood.

All Dried Up and Useless

Dried up and useless,
that's what the bitter mother said.
Childless spinsters,
all dried up and useless:
her flapper daughters that don't want
to bed any bluenose fella
to make their bodies *worth* something.

> "Am I not enough,
> a vessel for my breath
> just like any man?
> A single silver fox with his brandy and cards
> is hounded only by his hounds."

"Why are mugs considered complete
the moment they scream outside the womb?
Just for owning some floppy bits between their legs?"

> "My body is whole, and I breathe
> every day. I move about, interact, sleep.
> This *kitten* is a full human being, as is."

"You call us unaccomplished, Mother,
because children are all you accomplished."

> "You obeyed what you believed
> women are supposed to do,
> rather than follow the dreams
> we shebas realize instead."

"I never asked to be useful.
I never asked for a muff.
I exist from your whim
but I ankle by my own."

Worthless

I love my worthless womb
and my uselessness.
My existence was not my choice,
yet I'm glad to be

the end of all your hope.
Your joy is not my job.

Wanted

"What man wants you?"

My husband
Also doesn't want kids
Interrupting our sex

With temper tantrums over spilled milk,
Daddy smiled weird, their show isn't on,
A shadow passed the window,

They don't like carrots,
Mommy's iPhone is out of reach,
A glass shattered on the floor.

My husband
Also enjoys consequence-free
Life

And
Experiencing for the sake of experiencing
Fun.

No, we don't serve a purpose to you.
We never asked to serve a purpose—
I don't know how many times I keep saying this.

But you think we should
Because you think you should
So much you try, daily, exhausted,

And that's why
We're not miserable,
You are,

And that's why,
Painted in green,
You want us to be punished.

I Guess Serenity is Villainy Now

We're a pair of villains to your traditional mind
and honestly hon, to us, that's just fine.
Picture the fingernails our mothers made us
as vulture talons if you will, like failed mating harpies
searching to snatch your children in the night.
Of course we're jealous,
watching you live the life we never wanted.
So envious, yes,
of your daily screaming
because we'll never know love like it
—our less-than-human
lizard brains dictating tongues to dart
across each other's warmed skin.
Hedonistic heathens, so scary! With teeth
as dull as your own, gnashing
mixed greens and strawberries.
I'm feeling sleepy in this sun-drunk stupor
with no need to keep one eye open.

Becoming VILE

She lives like Carmen Sandiego in 1996:
knowledge thief with a VILE
villains' league of evil larceny,
secrets to steal to keep society second
guessing and silent like she was
always kept growing up, best in class
like some show dog, then knocked down
to knock up once prime beauty passed,
just like the other girls who came before.

Feral ferocity breaks free.

She gnashes her teeth then bites
the feeding hand holding her still,
rips off the leash and rolls
in newly discovered
$clay + silt + H_2O = mud$
to rub the pheromones off.
No pups would confine her mind
behind a white picket fence. Prison bars
pulse gray on closed eyelids. She runs.

So quickly she goes, back in time
to save the library of Alexandria
for her own rooms,
then sets fire to the building
to blame the true villains for its loss—
those who withheld its treasures
from hungry eyes untaught.

Left to gaze
upon a barren desert without distraction
in periphery, the sphinx never cried for its nose,
stolen by she to show the world how

power crumbles when particulates swarm
in just the right waft of warm air.
She strokes its shaft when deep in thought
within her vault, surrounded by axes and swords…
their absence led to missionaries' triumph,
and now she thinks to steal a Book once more.

The men aren't getting it. Time
for a little chaos with the absence
of their Freedom Declaration.
True tyranny is being born
in a body the world demands to use
for its own ends with no thought
or care for the owner within.
But steal their ideas; they'll write them again
and this time ensure illiterate mares
in wives who were meant for more.

Fine.

If you call her chaotic
when she holds linguistic sway—
watch her wild power when restrained.
Lock her in and she sneaks out the back,
leaving the gate open
for Pamplona bulls to escape.

Ask her for a glass of water
you can fetch all by yourself:
here's the Dead Sea purified
for Your Highness,
and you'll never find the salt again.
She wrecks environments in defiance.

She steals old writer's desks
where once was penned
sad servant sirens and seething succubi,

with no in-between. In such tales both
the subservient and the serpent
were man-eaters in the end.
To the bottom of the sea
go those watered-down details!
Some women don't live for men at all,
but you detest not being the protagonist.

The keys to the tower of London
are easily snatched and tossed down
an American wishing well
by this anarchist colonist.
Let hectic crime contend
with oppressive Parliament.

You like Lady Liberty
with her ever-glowing torch
welcoming the weary? So you say
as you turn them all away
with your alien accusations.
Well, now it's hers. You'll never find it—
but they will, those worldly women
looking for an underground escape
from your calloused clutches.
Her red coat is made of stretchy fabric
to keep them warm while you freeze
without the fire of an ally's gift.

With the rest of the Dead Sea water
that couldn't fit in your meager cup,
she makes dormant Mount Olympus,
source of the flame you stole
to burn the leaves growing
from Daphne's hair,
poor little laurel chased for beauty.
Poor little laurel
thought Father had made her body safe

but you kept battering her as tree
to reward the strength of her assailants.
Congratulate yourself
for this, Fool. Fooled, finally
by the one you deride.

She grins and between her teeth
Havana's famous cigars line up like trophies
taken straight from mobsters' mouths
in a rush of red barely seen by a blink.
At first, they thought their sight was stolen,
but when prismatic haze returned,
the serpentine smoke had cleared.

Around the Globe exist King's stages
where only men could be entertained
for the longest time. Even now it's all
male-made for the male gaze. She smiles
sardonically as she takes over
a Shakespearean landscape to lift Ophelia
where she belongs—above the water
climbing trees with the same muscled legs
any human has, and this time never to fall
in out of despair over a man.

The Uterus Desert

I'm not
sorry to disappoint you.
I love my Uterus desert
with the one oasis
only he can find—
a lake with no outlet
to the teeming ocean.
I'm not
a fish that you can catch

and really,
that's your problem, isn't it?

You Think I Should Kill Myself?

"Delete yourself and get out of the way…"

(Self) Murder is harm.
Not birthing is not harm.
Learn the difference
between action and inaction.

Babe, I'm already here
and people love me
and people would miss me,
but nobody can miss
who?
never existed.

Hypotheticals
don't have names
don't get graves
don't form bonds
don't feel love.

What Future Exactly?

"…because some of us actually care about the future."

The future
adding five pounds of trash to the planet
per person per day?

The future
adding to the influx of car exhaust
eating the ozone?

The future
adding to the already-competitive job market
that's phasing humans out in favor of AI?

No, the only future you care about
is your own bloodline, "making sure
the human race doesn't die out." (It won't.)

You certainly don't care about
the habitat harmed by humanity.
The Greater Good is human-centric, after all.

Conditional

Oh, Mama Bear—
your love requires
a blood bond, a genetic
tie so tight no knife can sever.
You prefer an extension of your-
self…less nothing, all You, You, You
plus one necessary to make it so.

You claim
real love is unconditional
while you bite your twisted tongue
to clarify why the blood of the womb
is thicker than that of the covenant
and forget it's all watered-
down Lucy. Dead hominid
no worthier or less than any living cousin.

I'd Rather Take an Arrow

I'd rather take an arrow to my belly button
than push it out from within.
I'd rather foster chocolate cake lipids
rounding me into an elephant ball
than moving arms of an entity I cannot see
stretching to rip my lungs apart
in search of its own breath.

The Myth of Freedom

Daedalus wanted it for Icarus.
He could have had it for himself.
Icarus seized it without question,
did not look back at the father
that saved him, though Father had expected
his baby would care once born. Icarus flew
for one breath, knowing what birds feel,
but Apollo scolded his desire,
enforcing Promethean design
for man to toil the mud he comes from
some decades before returning below.
Minds dream of more beyond
the families and species they are born to
but never achieve it, imprisoned in restrictive flesh.

Disposal

Battered bones gray,
weathered with age
and raw beatings by the waves,
slowly sink to sand, forever to sleep
under the crushing weight of water
until a hiding stingray's wing-fins flip
the fragments into a passing shark's wake.
Bottled water left microscopic plastics
embedded in the calcium:
fossilization in the Anthropocene.

Reduce
Reuse
Recycle

Decompose in compost…but no.
Consumerism makes trash out of convenience,
and car-crash corpses invade the sea the same.
Polystyrene coats Sapien tongues in foam
peanut pebbles bubbling from gaping mouths.
They do not sink soaked but float and fly
through the saltwater like little beads
to fool the blue whales of a krill breakfast
that comes just in time for a death knell.

Reduce
Reuse
Recycle

Thousands of pounds of shit leftover from life
(litter, diapers, and doggie bags)
all meditate in the city dump,
percolating with rainwater
to become leachate in the ocean.

Reduce
Reuse
Recycle

What is homeostasis to industrial aliens
who will never relive their native ape days?

Reduce
Reuse
Recycle

Equilibrium, annihilated. Even healers harm.
A virus can only be cured when the multiplying stops.

The Birds

My single prayer, if any gods are listening, is
for the birds to take over,
to Hitchcock for their inheritance;
for the crows to caw triumphant
in the wake of our corpses;
for the raptors to reign again and damn the asteroid
that never should have hit,
that hit too soon.

Slurs

Old Maid
Cat Lady
Crone
Spinster
Surplus Woman
Sheng nu…

Her unused uterus
is such a threat
that you must tease,
bully with names
to hide your fear
of a woman defined
by something other
than her portal.

How? She lives
the life given her,
rather than erase herself,
rather than give it up
to a stranger,
rather than replicate
the same-old sacrifice
of her mother's mother.

When a man does the same,
he is merely called
a golden bachelor,
a silver fox.

Why is his pristine seed
off-limits?
Where is his
derogatory epithet?

Is he not guilty
of the same damn crime?

Crabs in the Bucket

Pincers have plenty to pinch when it comes to my ass.
Frustrated crabs push violin bows into my cheek dimples.
They number multitudes, to swell the melody
Of, "child-bearing hips, what a shame."

The crustaceans claw at the lines of their own faces
And mimic crows' incessant jabber to peck me down to size
Claiming my size is that of a multiparous mother and
I shouldn't be childfree if I don't look the part.

My same years have left me with smooth skin.
They can't have that!
Chittering that my lack of laugh lines means I never laugh;
So miserable I must be without the love of littles

As though I don't have the love of others at all.
They whimper the same chorus, over and over again,
To make me memorize their misery as my own
Loneliness, to make me believe I need their lives

To fit in and understand the love that transcends
Screams and diaper blow-outs and underdeveloped brain
Selfishness—perfectly valid to entertain
When it comes from a mind I made, rather than my own.

They do try, I'll give them credit for the effort,
But their pincers feel like gnats crawling on thin hairs.
One little smack sends them flying, jolted and twisted,
Easily cracked for the salty boil.

Final Destination

every family will have a final descendant.
i've simply chosen to be mine.

a final juddering escalator
ride
down a darkened mall
pinch
a final soot-stained hand
crawl
up cold chimney bricks
fall
a final bicycle wheel
swing
against a growing pine
crash
a final highway car
chase
by tired traffic cops
plummet
a final weakened prey
sneak
through a growling wood
gnash

a final earthquake
a final tornado
a final hurricane
a final sirocco
a final roller coaster
a final plane crash
a final gun shot
a final knife
a final stroke
a final heart attack

a final funeral

a final coffin

then no one left
to reverently bury the final body
before the sun burns
the grass to ash
and
the NiFe core to hydrogen.

a final burning plasma ball
resets the match.
a new game begins
without humans to play.
oh, sweetie, there's no such thing
as immortality.

This Bloodline Dies with Me

i met my great-grandma at her funeral.
i don't know her mother's name.

what is legacy
when lineage is the word
and what is lineage
but weak knots in a severed string
decomposing in the grass,
forgotten to the sun.

and what is legacy, really
but inheritance
of someone else's accomplishments
babies don't have to work for to reap,
only to end up at the Reaper's door
after all.

Naysay

I didn't want to be this way,
but they all say I have to pay
for the weight of my unchosen days...

...a life overlain with frames now frayed
around flanks flayed and on display
by wary neighbors ashamed in vain.
Plain stares and baneful dares
led astray the jaywalkers of May.

My childhood age despised change,
but I came away to emancipate
the little lady I never hailed: break
praying faces prone by waning lakes
and embrace a crone's coat of gray.

Save this shade of Hades' disgrace,
for she awaits inflamed cold veins
and the fading hate of brain's decay.

Our Goddamn First-World Legacy

Of course animals win the game
and outbreed by instinct.
What do you think humans are
but advanced thinkers, beyond urge?
I can see how far our tools have come and
gone:
I want us to be....

If offspring will only lead to industry
and the Christians
who think humans own the world
like a fucking gift purchased by Jesus
to do with whatever they please—
if they are the breeders
and the hippies can't keep up;
if we can never go back
to unity with nature;
if we will only ever conquer
ourselves
into self-destruction,

let's begin now.
Everyone birth less
and give our home
a fighting chance to start over.

Leave the instinct of reproduction
to the biome we have never helped.

Appendix A: The Natural State of Things

Childlessness is the natural state of the body. A uterus cannot become pregnant until an outside agent (whether penis-in-vagina sex or IVF) invades. Someone else has to act upon the female form to form a baby. Sure, it is the natural progression of life to procreate, and my body has the capacity to gestate, but it doesn't do so inherently. We are not asexual reproducers, and therefore a choice exists whether to reproduce at all.

Childlessness is necessary for population control in a species that has no natural predators what with our advanced technology, improved medicine, and artificial habitats. There's this circle of life humans have exempted themselves from yet insist on participating in. Look at the natural food chain—there are fewer predators than prey. This ensures both populations can be maintained and flourish. But humans have to manipulate our resources to maintain us all. The earth's natural resources just can't keep up with our numbers. And because of medicine extending longevity, there are more people existing at the same time than there has ever been.

Voluntary childlessness is good for the planet, not the least because it reduces trash, carbon emissions, and habitat destruction. In its choice exists the feeling of pure freedom, hence the term we have adopted and the name of this book: child*free*. However, when involuntary, it is pitiable. I believe one hundred percent that people should be able to plan their families and live their lives how they want. I've often said if the universe were fair, all women who want babies would be fertile, while infertility would befall only the childfree. It would therefore be seen as a bonus rather than a defect, and would dramatically reduce the number of abortions.

When I was a child, I did think I'd have children. "Someday, when I grow up, I'll have two or three." I was given baby dolls and taught that it was the natural progression of adulthood: go to school, get a job, get married, have kids. It was an undefined, amoebous future that I didn't really think too hard about until the marriage happened. My husband and I were still very poor starting out, even with a combined income, so we knew we wanted to delay kids. But the more I thought about it, the more I didn't want to be pregnant. I hated everything about the concept. The parasitic nature of the fetus scared me to death. I just cannot separate pregnancy from parasitism. The fact that the fetus will steal nutrients from the mother's own body if she doesn't get enough is absolutely horrifying. The body prioritizes the fetus's life over its own. Absolutely horrifying. And then the responsibility of keeping a baby alive, and the possibility of jail if the mother fails and it dies. Not to mention when I imagined a child calling me "Mommy," it felt all kinds of wrong. I didn't want to do it. One day it just clicked—I didn't have to. I felt free…until I received pushback from others for saying no. I was perplexed. My husband and I agreed, so what did it matter?

Honestly, after years of condemnation, I'm not surprised anymore that society perceives the childfree negatively. There's a reason villains are frequently childless and queer-coded. We are the deviants, the ones who buck tradition, the threats to the natural order. We're "going against God." We aren't openly showing, through the simple existence of a(n expected) relationship, that we are self-sacrificing, generous, "good" people (never mind that there are neglectful and abusive parents). We critique, we question, we choose a different path, and that confuses people. And what people don't understand, they fear.

Appendix B: I Still Have to Center Children

I don't like the phrase "childless by choice," because the word *less* implies that having children is the default, automatic condition. The default status of my uterus is empty. I'm born with it empty, I live most (all) of my life with it empty.

Children only occur with the intervention of sperm. It takes the involvement of another person to initiate the process of a child's formation.

Mothers are child-*full*. I'm just me. Yet womanhood is so inextricably entwined with motherhood that we are forced to define our lifestyle by the negative of our uterus usage: we are *child*-free, *child*-less, non-*mothers*. When I left the Christian cult I was raised in, I wasn't stuck calling myself "ex-Christian" or "non-Christian." I had a lexicon of beliefs and labels to discover and try on, so that I wasn't trapped defining myself by what I was not.

The childfree don't have a word that is inherently positive. There are a few terms for childless women, but these are focused on pre-sexual states (maiden, virgin), as though once a woman has sex, pregnancy and birth are imminent and inevitable. Words for non-breeding animals exist but are demeaning to use for a person. "Heifer" comes to mind.

I'm okay with *childfree*. The freedom is the best positive spin we can put on it to show our satisfaction. But it's still frustrating that I have to center children in any way to my identity.

Appendix C: My Purpose

"Without kids, what is your purpose?"

What is my purpose here? A certain pirate sent me to settle his debt.

But seriously, you spay and neuter your pets. What is their purpose to you? To bring you joy and companionship and emotional support, right? That's what I do for my friends, my husband, the patients I listen to, the doctors I serve.

Why is this question always directed at (presumed) women? Men have careers and hobbies, some don't end up having children, and rarely are they asked what their purpose was.

Also, why do I need a purpose to continue existing? My parents created me. It's not like I volunteered to be here. I didn't say, "Please bring me into this world so I can be a mother myself." I didn't have any plan, direction, or goal when she pushed me out of her womb. My only obligation as a living, breathing mammal is just that. To breathe. To eat, shit, and sleep. To stay alive because my instinct tells me to.

My reproductive instinct, however, has been suppressed, because the advanced intelligence that comes with being human has taught me that genetic immortality is not real immortality. I will die regardless of all factors. My consciousness will cease to be. I cannot live within the people I might create. Witnessing how badly humans have impacted the planet tells me our species' perpetuation is not essential, and decreasing the population might actually help the quality of all creatures' lives.

Animals do not know that they will die. That is the crucial difference between us. Knowing our deaths are inevitable influences religion and holy wars, scientific research, and our personal priorities. I know my time is limited. I will spend it on activities and media and people that uplift me, nourish my soul, and inform my mind, to be my best self. I will not start over at my beginning with someone brand new. For me, that is going backward. I want to go forward.

My personal path is my purpose. I don't need to be useful to you.

Appendix D: So Many Reasons

At the time of formatting *Nulligravida*, I thought it would look neat to have my Reasons and Answers sprinkled at various points throughout the book between poems, out of order. I thought of it as a game for readers to see if they could find all (at the time) 40 reasons, or if they thought I was randomly assigning numbers that didn't actually equal the total. I know better now. No one put in that effort, and the chaos of the format was only distracting. This time, I am including my list as an addendum, so the poetry can stand alone for what it is. Note that this list is in no particular order.

1) I *hate* the sound of a crying baby. It makes me cringe.

2) Children are noisy, selfish, and dependent. They can't help it, but I can help having that in my life.

3) I can't stand being around people for any extended period, so why would I make more? Especially one that will be a leech on my time and money and never leave me alone. I need time to myself to think and play and recharge, and children are basically always in your face. No "off" button. I would never be alone again for 20+ years.

4) I understand all organisms must breed to keep life on Earth perpetual, existence *ad infinitum*. But I am too self-aware. My heredity, my health, the innate "nature" part of my personality—these are not worth remaining longer than my own years.

5) I don't want to give my relatives more relatives or reasons to insert themselves into my life. I am not proud of my DNA and have no longing to see it immortalized. I don't want my family's influence, no matter how slight.

There are individuals in my family that are racist, homophobic, arrogant, right-fighting conspiracy theorists, and once upon a time they tried to mold me in that image. Nope.

6) My father is deceased, but his arrogance, violence, and stubbornness live in me. I'm not dealing with that genetic makeup in a child.

7) My eyesight is not something I want to pass on. My husband's migraines are not something I want to pass on. My husband and I are both introverts, likely to create one, and unfortunately, society is tailored for extraverts. My child would be born with multiple disadvantages.

8) The exorbitant cost of vision care and glasses. I work in optometry and know why the prices are the way they are, but that knowledge doesn't change the (un)affordability.

9) I am terrible about keeping up with annual physician appointments, which my kid would require. Not to mention I hate speaking on the phone and detest confrontation of any kind.

10) My husband's unhealthy diet would instigate fights over family dinner, leading to resentment. And I would likely resent him in general because I already do all the chores, so who do you think would be caring for the kids?

11) The majority of divorces happen after the couple reproduces. Mostly due to resentment (e.g. one parent isn't helping enough with the children, one parent isn't pulling their weight with the household income, neither adult is available for sex anymore, leading to infidelity…). I'm not taking that risk.

12) The longevity of my marriage is due to our dedication to one another without a child to distract us from the relationship. It's weird to me when people are surprised "you've lasted this long when you don't have kids," as if...what? By my observation, people who say this tend to have kids because they started to hate each other and were trying to fix their relationship. So I guess they're surprised we haven't started to hate each other? Are they surprised we've been together so many years without needing to create a whole-ass new human as a Band-Aid? I don't understand these people any more than they understand me. I don't need to stay motivated to "stick it out" or "overcome our differences" with the inconvenience a child would bring. I don't want to demote him or be demoted. I don't want to resent him over childcare. I love him and want to focus on him forever.

13) It alarms me how a woman's body changes during and after pregnancy. Thinking about the process and the damage is nauseating. I am physically sickened by the idea and look of a pregnant belly. The concept of a parasitic entity moving around inside me is revolting. I don't want to experience my vagina stretching to accommodate the baby's body (just the thought of that is nauseating). The fact that vaginal birth can cause a perineal tear to the anus (and the fact there's a procedure called an episiotomy to tear it *safely*) terrifies me. Also, a third- or fourth-degree tear requires surgical repair of the muscles, right after birth. I am horrified.

14) I don't exercise enough as it is, so knowing I could likely never get rid of the weight gain (especially from my already-DDD breasts) is extremely unappealing. Yes, I'm vain.

15) My sister and cousin had preeclampsia, and I have hypertension already. I have a higher risk of death from something I don't even want and have a choice not to endure.

16) My mother has had bladder and rectal prolapses in her elderly years from birth-induced injury to her pelvic floor. I'd rather not have to deal with that pain and medical expense.

17) Breast milk. Even if I didn't breastfeed, I would still have to pump it out because I'd be producing it. The smell is disgusting....

18) Lactating accidents in the shower and around crying babies is a thing. Gross.

19) Not saying I will, because I won't, but if I do change my mind too late, I can adopt. I'd rather feed a hungry mouth than create a new hungry mouth. I don't understand the desire for genetic immortality when there are orphans who need loving parents. Having your own child is selfish.

20) Expensive! We're barely affording life as it is. Adding a child and its insurances, food, clothes...car later, and college fund.... We can't do it.

21) Project supplies, holiday gift expectations, phone upgrades for the whole family, computers and tablets...

22) The stress of driving lessons. The inevitable accident(s) and extraneous new car purchase.

23) Every parent I overhear (not talk to, because most parents try to manipulate the childfree into thinking parenthood is wonderful) is maximally stressed. Some

even tell their kids they are burdens, and say, "just wait until you have your own," as if it is a punishment and their children have no choice. I'm not inviting that extra stress into my life if I can help it.

24) Bingos. Those relentless, repetitive questions from parents insinuating my choice is wrong. The more parents repeat themselves, the less I want children.

25) I just don't want them. I have almost no nurturing instinct, and that's nature controlling overpopulation. We have few predators, so instincts have had to morph to keep the balance.

26) Where this world is heading sucks. Political and religious extremists, technology eliminating jobs, both killing the planet. I'm not leaving progeny to deal with this.

27) Having to listen to, "Can I have this?" one hundred times in one shopping trip, and the subsequent temper tantrum when I say No.

28) Kids are, by nature, clumsy and rambunctious, and would break at least one of my delicate glasses or collectibles. I know because I did.

29) The Category 5 hurricane detritus of vomit and poop and scattered toys Mommy has to clean up on a daily basis. I don't want that chaos, ever.

30) Without kids, I won't have to cook or do laundry as frequently. Laziness is a poor reason, but it's one of many.

31) With no kids, there is no loss of income from staying home more often or quitting my job. No sacrificing my

career goals. No sacrificing the full capabilities of my mind.

32) With no kids, I don't have to relive basic education and don't have to tolerate nursery rhymes or kid's shows. I can continue to learn and educate myself beyond the college level, to be the best I can be, rather than start over teaching a child the basics.

33) I don't want to create a new person until I am self-actualized, which may never happen—there is always more to learn and discover.

34) I don't want to add to the masses and encourage low-quality production. "Lowest cost, highest number" is corporations' motto to get product in consumer hands, and this is causing tacky work and planned obsolescence. If the population decreases by fewer births, quality should become priority again.

35) I will not subject another life to be falsely accused and unfairly punished because of the liars and cheaters in the world, or create a life that is a liar/cheater.

36) My mother is my kid...she's becoming frail and is all alone. I don't want the crushing depression that she had from caring for her widowed mom and infant daughter. And my mother-in-law is not nurturing. So basically, I'd have no "mothering" help, with multiple "infants."

37) It takes a village to raise a child. I have no village. The family circle is so small and fractured that I can confidently say I would have no help. My father is dead, my mother is dying, my sister has two autistic kids of her own, my other sister lives across the country, my sister-in-law has her hands full as a nurse with two boys of her own, my father-in-law has health problems that preclude

childcare. Even my friends are either moving away to start their own families or dealing with crushing anxiety and depression.

38) After monthly mortgage payments and bills, my husband and I have zero money left for the exorbitant cost of daycare. I don't want kids as it is, but logistically, I couldn't make it work even if I did want them.

39) I've heard stories of teenagers stealing their mom's credit cards to buy expensive frivolous shit online. I never did that, but it's entirely possible that my kids might. Even if I teach them not to lie or steal, lessons don't always stick, especially at that age...I don't want to risk it.

40) The attitude. There is no guarantee that the kid will grow up to like or even love me. No guarantee it will help or care. Estranged behavior after all the stress and effort to form and raise it into a functioning adult would be devastating.

41) My kid would be involved in bullying (bully or victim) which I would then have to deal with. Too much stress and responsibility. I know myself well enough to know I could not handle it.

42) Having to help with (do) kids' school projects.

43) Having to listen to jealousy of their peers' upbringing. ("But Renee gets to do it! But Taylor has one!")

44) Having to deal with inconsistent correction ("Daddy said I could!") and the resulting resentment of my spouse.

45) I am saddened to see what advancing technology is doing to education. Even elementary-school-age children are using computers and tablets, staring at screens for hours basically from infancy. Schools aren't bothering to teach kids how to tell analog time or write cursive. Yes, I could teach my children this on my own, but it's the principle of the thing. Even my own memory has suffered from an overreliance on internet search engines.

46) Part of my revulsion for childbearing and rearing has to do with my individuality and distaste for being told what to do and what to think. One of the most irritating bingos to me is the reaction of shock: "That's just what you do, it's the next step of life, it's natural. You're a woman, you have maternal instinct and a biological clock, how can you not feel that...? You're not an adult until you have kids." It just makes me reject the idea even more.

47) It's very likely I'd have to start asking my husband's permission to spend money, since there would be some length of time that I'd be a stay-at-home mom. That's not okay; we both appreciate having an independent percentage of our separate incomes to spend on whatever we want without deferring to the other person.

48) My family has opposite political and religious views from me, views that are very restrictive. I would have to supervise every visit and never let them babysit because they would confuse the child with harmful ideas.

49) The amount of trash I generate alone nauseates me. The amount of waste we accept as a society nauseates me. We are litter embodied, a virus on this planet. I cannot ethically consciously duplicate my species to further kill

our habitat. The environment and other animals have more right to exist than our human disease.

50) I despise the assumption that because I have breasts, I'm inherently nurturing and can look after someone else's kid if they leave the room. I don't know what to do with a kid. I would freeze and panic if it got into trouble. I am, simply, not the mothering type.

51) I was put on this earth as a witness, to participate as little as possible in order to observe my surroundings with minimal interference. I was made to feel like an alien in this environment for a reason.

52) I am repulsed by the notion of strangers touching my stomach, asking questions, being intrusive, and thinking I'm rude for not wanting to talk about my private business.

53) I have become exactly what parents expect of their children: a caregiver. I have come to resent this role and my mother, whom I thought I loved. I will not do this to hypothetical children. I will not create a whole new person to be my keeper when I am old. I will not place such an expectation, a burden, on someone who did not ask to exist.

54) I can barely balance my life now to the point of satisfaction. Between my job, my husband, my elderly mother for whom I am the main caretaker...none of this is optional. Add the necessity of friends for emotional support and the downtime an introvert like me requires recuperating from responsibilities, and I just don't have time for kids. I just don't.

55) I have observed narcissistic tendencies in almost all my family members: my mother, her mother, my father and

his sisters, his parents…and me. As the daughter of a narcissistic mother, I refuse to become one myself. Even this self-awareness will not help me avoid falling into that genetic instinct, and I refuse to abuse another person in that way.

56) No, my childhood was not perfect in regard to relationships, but I loved and feel nostalgic for the media and entertainment I grew up with. I love the media and entertainment I have now. Some of what I consume now includes graphic violence, swearing, and sexuality. I enjoy the art for what it is and will not hide it away "for the sake of my child." There is no child. I can continue to peruse and learn adult-oriented content as I evolve as an individual, while at the same time extend my adolescence through entertainment when I come home from work. Relaxation and amusement are important to balance life and reduce stress. I will not prematurely age. I will not repress my interests. And I don't need to have a child to re-live my childhood when nostalgia strikes.

57) I never thought I'd become the older generation intimidated by new technologies, but the sudden emergence of AI scares me. I don't want to create a child who might use AI to cheat on homework and thereby never learn on their own (especially when it comes to critical thinking). I don't want a hypothetical child to be manipulated and fooled by AI-generated images. By the time the hypothetical child is old enough to use AI, who knows how advanced it will be? I am thoroughly distressed at how AI is already usurping real writers and artists now in 2025. We've gone too far.

58) While I would teach a hypothetical child social justice and tolerance, there is no guarantee it would hold on to those lessons. Even with parental blocks, I can't control what the child would hear from peers at school or what

websites or content creators the child would come across to change its mind. My parents raised me a conservative Christian, but thanks to the Internet, I opened my mind, progressed, and became a liberal agnostic pagan. I went from "I am right, you are wrong," to "Live and let live." If I was able to do that in the 2010s, I can't imagine what will be accessible for a child in the years to come. I will not risk a hypothetical child going backwards and potentially becoming an intolerant "tradwife" or evangelical or white supremacist or incel or MRA.

59) The rapid increase in gun violence in schools is terrifying. I will not raise a victim or perpetrator. I refuse to risk that.

60) [Formerly the essay "My Mentality"]
Mitigating my anxiety is more necessary and valuable to me than having kids. I can barely take care of myself as it is, and strangers want me to procreate simply because my body *has a uterus*? My incredulity knows no bounds.
   a. I was not "put here" to have a kid. If I were, this god they speak of would have put the desire in me. I was "put here" to experience life in whatever form my own instinct determines. I will not apologize for defying my societal "duty."
   b. As humans have evolved, we have expanded our intelligence to find many new opportunities to spend our time. Simple survival through genetic proliferation is the purview of animals with nothing else to do. I am not calling parents animals, don't misunderstand me; I am saying that those who see procreation as their sole purpose—the end—are undervaluing their human experience.

   c.   I just want acknowledgement and tolerance. You want kids? Fine. I don't want kids? Also fine.

61) Mammal physiology grosses me out. I know, I need therapy, my head examined, I'm what's wrong with women these days. Whatever. Growing offspring *inside* and feeding the result with our own bodies feels like parasitic cannibalism. Maybe I was a lizard in a past life. Maybe I'll be a snake in the next. Que será, será. I like breathing and my warm blood, but if I think about it too hard, I really hate my body.

Appendix E: Answers to Common Questions (Bingos)

I don't want children. I just don't. That should be enough. But people keep wasting their breath, so here we go…

- I do know true love. I have a dog.

- I don't care that I'm missing out.

- I would be a terrible mother.

- On that note, how do you know I would be a good mother? You barely know my name. What are you basing that on—my boobs?

- I don't want to know, and I don't care, how "my own" would be different.

- Why would you wish children into a home where they're unwanted? You realize there are mothers who abandon and surrender their infants? How are you so certain I wouldn't be one of them? I'm pretty certain I would. It's better not to find out.

- The same assisted living facility your kids will put you in, and I'll have money to pay for it.

- Eight billion people haven't cured cancer. Including you. And your mother had such high hopes that you would be the One.

- The biological clock is a false metaphor created in the 1970s to dissuade career women. And it's not ticking. I had a better use for the batteries.

- Curiosity in a hypothetical child's appearance is a terrible reason to reproduce. Children are not dolls.

- The "new baby smell" is the sweet decay of rotten eggs and stale Cheerios. I'll pass.

- I'm not a real adult? So, can you tell my body to stop aging and then dying? Because that would be awesome.

- If my parents hadn't had me, we wouldn't be having this conversation and I wouldn't know the difference.

- Having been a baby once is irrelevant. I was not responsible for myself.

- It's *selfish* to reproduce your own DNA instead of adopting one of the thousands of orphans and surrendered kids in the foster system. Making sure you have "your own," means it's still all about you: your blood, your genes, your lineage.

- There is no soul waiting for me to be its mother. If there were, I'd have the desire.

- No. The Bible claims God said that when there was (supposedly) a grand total of two people in existence. There are now eight billion. Let's skip a year. Also: Jesus was childfree.

- Just because I don't want kids doesn't mean everyone doesn't want kids.

- The human race will not die out. Maybe it should? The pollution and carbon dioxide one person generates over their lifetime, even if that person is environmentally conscious, is sickening. The Earth will survive without humanity.

- Children are a woman's greatest achievement, but not a man's? I have the same mental capacity as a man.

- Children are not The Reason for marriage. Marriage provides a life-long witness to your life, the love of a peer, and financial support when your dependence on parents ends. Marriage is the government recognizing your partnership as a family.

- My family name is poison. My husband does not care that his family name will belong to his cousins.

- "Genetic immortality" is absurd; my dead father cannot see through my myopic eyes. I refuse to reproduce my inherited health conditions.

- What part of "I like my life and I don't want it to change" equates to "I was abused and depressed as a child"? Actually, my childhood was so fun that my life goal is Extended Adolescence, with a bare minimum of adult responsibility (just enough to appease my societal role of stimulating the economy, and surviving, by having a job).

- Childfree people of childbearing age, if they were jealous of you, would simply have a child! Whereas childless people would if they could, making it extremely cruel to tell them that they're jealous and bitter. So who exactly are you preaching to?
  - o I know, it's other regretful parents. You're the ones jealous that the childfree community is eluding the responsibility you thought was required in life, and to make yourselves feel better about your burden, you spread lies about

our mental states. You hate that we get to have fewer stressors (not no stress, part of Being Alive is stress, no matter your lifestyle).

- You don't know I'm not infertile. How can you be so careless about something so sensitive and personal?

- No, I won't change my mind.

Appendix F: The Grandchild Bingo

"But doesn't your mom want grandkids?"

"But grandkids could become so important to you later in life! Won't you feel like you're missing out?"

Having children so they'll give you grandchildren is selfish and misguided. You're operating under the assumption you can predict and dictate what another human does with their life. You're setting yourself up for disappointment and a strained relationship if they don't meet your expectations. Kids are not pre-programmed machines. They will not turn out according to your script no matter how you raise them. Let them become who they determine. Maybe that's childfree. Love them for who they are, not who you want them to be.

"But you don't have kids; how dare you tell us what to think!"

Correct.

I'm not speaking from a parent's perspective.

I'm speaking from the child's perspective.

I know what that pressure is like. It doesn't stop just because I grew up.

Questions like the ones above seem to come from self-involved individuals who believe theirs is the only personality type that exists. Since they feel like they'd miss having grandkids, those who choose not to are making A Mistake.

Not everyone has a personality that enjoys small children. I have inherited from my mother severe episodic anxiety that causes heart palpitations, dizziness, and high blood pressure, which happens with overexposure to many and/or loud people.

Little children are shrill and hyper, and while I appreciate people who find it cute and enjoyable, I do not.

Appreciate my existence also.

Some of us enjoy being alone. Trust me, I'm not lonely.

My mother is happy I'm not having kids since I am her live-in caretaker and living with a baby would drive her up the wall.

My experiences are valid. To dismiss them because I'm "not a parent" is an excuse not to listen to my advice. I can't make you have an open mind. That's your prerogative. But please, stop the false concern and faux outrage just because you're confused that I dare deviate from the Life Script™.

Acknowledgements

This has been, for the most part, a private labor of love, however there are a few friends I want to thank, and some strangers.

First, a special thanks to Marcia Drut-Davis, paving the way for childfree acceptance since her 60 Minutes interview in 1974. You are the elderly guru I aspire to become.

To childfree influencers Kimberly (Childfree Kimberly), Marcela (Childfree Millennial), and Jade (Childfree Living), who tirelessly post about childfree and childless acceptance on YouTube and Instagram: your encouragement, support, and positivity for our community is so important to combat the criticism and slander from unhappy parents who would rather harbor anger towards us online than take care of their kids. Thank you for creating a safe space for like-minded people to connect.

To my husband: thank you for putting up with me! For leaving me alone when I ask, for keeping me company when I ask, for your suggestions as a reader, and for the shoulder massages at the computer. *We* are a family, just the two of us, and I love you so much.

To Hailey, Makenna, and Alice: thank you for sticking by my side. Thank you for understanding me. Thank you for the laughter, for the hugs, for the tea, for the cat chats. You came into my life right when I needed you, and I am forever grateful.

To my unrequited crushes in high school who thought I was ugly, and the one who said I was like a sister: thank you for keeping me from a teen pregnancy. I didn't realize it then, but you did me a huge favor by rejecting me.

To the doctor who performed my bilateral salpingectomy, who will remain nameless here for legal and privacy reasons: I am grateful for your dedication to support not only the health of women, but their agency as well. To paraphrase what you told me at our first meeting when I brought up sterilization: "I want to avoid paternalism in medicine. I am not your father, and besides, you are an adult. My job is to inform you about your body and your choices, not make that choice for you. It's your body, and your life. I don't care about the question of regret. If you regret it, that's on you."

Damn right, doc.

About the Author

Saralyn Caine is a feminist poet and cat lady living on the outskirts of the Great Dismal Swamp. When not writing, her crone spirit can be found haunting the cypress trees and singing softly to the moon—though her husband would prefer she finish her tea first. Caine has been published by *The Poet's Haven Digest*, *Arlington Literary Journal*, and *Quillkeepers Press*. She is the author of poetry collections *Magic & Mayhem*, *Nulligravida*, *The Soul Without a Summer*, and *Honey Eaters*.

Find her online at saralyncainepoetry.com